THE SECRET AN W9-CUT-947

Dr. William R. Parker, Professor at California's University of Redlands and author of this book, found himself on the verge of a nervous breakdown. When other help failed he began to pray, and in a few months he was well again.

Fascinated by the power of prayer, Dr. Parker conducted an experiment, in which forty-five men and women—including agnostics, a minister, and an atheist—shed their worldly troubles and developed a triumphant new method of self-help: Prayer Therapy.

"Over and over," writes Dr. Parker, "we proved that whatever we had need of, whether it was harmony, forgiveness, courage, abundance, friendship, health, if we would affirm it and accept it within, it would become a part of our outward experience. This was both the secret and the miracle."

PRAYER CAN CHANGE YOUR LIFE
was originally published by Prentice-Hall, Inc.

PRAYER CAN CHANGE YOUR LIFE

Experiments and Techniques in Prayer Therapy

By William R. Parker
and Elaine St. Johns

PUBLISHED BY POCKET BOOKS NEW YORK

PRAYER CAN CHANGE YOUR LIFE

Prentice-Hall edition published 1957

POCKET BOOK edition published June, 1974

3rd printing .... October, 1974

L

This POCKET BOOK edition includes every word contained in the original, higher-priced edition. It is printed from brand-new plates made from completely reset, clear, easy-to-read type. POCKET BOOK editions are published by POCKET BOOKS, a division of Simon & Schuster, Inc., 630 Fifth Avenue, New York, N.Y. 10020. Trademarks registered in the United States and other countries.

Standard Book Number: 671-78372-6.
Library of Congress Catalog Card Number: 57-6777.
Cover art by Terry McKee.

Printed in the U.S.A.

This book is gratefully dedicated to

The Original Prayer Therapy Group,
Those fifteen volunteer "guinea pigs"
Whose pioneer efforts in testing and validating
The power of prayer helped make this book possible.

CONTENTS

INTRODUCTION

PRAYER CAN CHANGE YOUR LIFE ANYTIME, ANYWHERE, at any age. It can heal your diseases, renew your mind and body, calm the storms of daily living from the great tempests of fear and sorrow that threaten to overwhelm —to the day by day squalls in human relationships that constantly rock our boat until we view a world distorted by a seasick haze.

These are not sweet words nor a Valentine philosophy. I have proven this truth in my own personal experience beyond the shadow of a doubt. I can say with authority that, if you can and will follow the simple techniques set down here, you can prove it in yours. The measure of the help you can get through prayer is limited only by the size of the cup you hold up to be filled.

Repeatedly, under scientific test conditions, divorced from incense or high emotional persuasion, I have seen its beneficial results. In the searching light of the classroom we have experimented with prayer under conditions satisfying all the demands of modern "scientific" man.

Our investigations yielded a Key. The Key opened the door to specific techniques, and through those techniques we were able to prove that prayer is not simply a supplement to other forms of treatment, a crutch to

11

build courage, but can be the most important tool in the reconstruction and rehabilitation of man's personality.

Translated those expensive academic words simply say again: "Prayer can change your life!"

During the ten years of our experiments at the University of Redlands we proved that prayer brings renewal, rebirth, that men and women *can* receive "beauty for ashes," release from fears, depression, discouragement, marital difficulties. Dramatic physical healings resulted when stuttering, arthritis, migraine headache, high blood pressure responded to the power of prayer. A professor retired because of tuberculosis returned to teaching. A woman who had undergone surgery to remove a pressure point on her brain, only to have epileptic seizures continue, found complete freedom during the course of our class.

Even more encouraging than these spectacular recoveries were the day to day adjustments to life, the "life more abundantly," the joy and peace achieved *right where they were* by individuals who had been convinced that nothing short of a million dollars, the prompt removal of a mother-in-law, a new husband, or a geographic cure (preferably in the neighborhood of Paris or Rome) could make their lives into a truly satisfying experience.

To those released from nervous anxieties and fears, it seemed miraculous to discover the Kingdom of Heaven exactly where Jesus of Nazareth had said it was, and is, within. Our Key put each man's enjoyment of life into his own keeping, a great release from the strain and frustration of constantly having to worry or win it from another—to outmaneuver or outwit some outside agency into granting us our good.

We called the combination of this Key, with specific prayer techniques, Prayer Therapy. The purpose of this book is to reveal the Key, detail our experiments and show precisely how prayer was applied to individual problems by following the directions of the successful prayers of the past. Actual names have been withheld, but the cases are factual. There is no escaping our results. Prayer Therapy worked for us. It could work for you.

If you are praying and experiencing no corresponding uplift in your joy, peace, appreciation of life, you are "praying amiss." This fact we came to accept without any self-condemnation when our initial experiment gave strong indications that the same can truthfully be said of much of the Christian world. The potential of prayer has been constant for the past 2000 years. Jesus of Nazareth, the most successful prayer who ever lived, and the Master Teacher accepted by all Christians, laid down certain rules or principles. He said that, from them, certain results would be attained. Life more abundantly; the peace that passeth understanding; healing; wholeness; fullness of joy; abiding love.

For a short time following His ministry His disciples (or students) continued to pray with signs following. But somewhere an error seemed to creep in between the principle and the practice. The answers weren't as dependable. The results weren't there.

If we dare to look around us today without the blinkers of superstition we might arrive at one of several views on prayer. It doesn't seem to be doing such a good job. There is too little peace, joy, more abundant life. Explanations vary: (1.) Prayer is a delusion and doesn't work at all; (2.) Prayer doesn't work on principle but by dispensation of a whimsical power which plays favorites and can be bribed . . . sometimes; (3.) People don't pray; (4.) They are praying amiss.

Our experiments proved the first three absolutely false and the fourth quite generally true. We were reminded that the Master's own students never once asked Him how to perform miracles, how to multiply loaves and fishes, find gold in a fish's mouth, raise the dead, convenient as this knowledge would have been. Instead they made one request: "Teach us to pray."

That was where our class started. Certainly, in the beginning, not one among us was a prayer expert.

No one can truthfully say prayer is not his business. Prayer is everyone's business. Properly understood, it becomes the focal point of individual life. Someone has said, "You are what you eat." We discovered "you are what you pray," whether you know it or not. What Hitler did was his prayer. What Albert Schweitzer did was his prayer. But prayer was not a part of my profession.

By profession, I am a college professor, a psychologist, a speech pathologist. In our speech clinic I was very definitely interested in healing but, until our experiments, I had no more than average interest in the connection between healing and prayer.

I attended church, dutiful if not devout. I prayed, conventionally, rather as a mark of respect than with the expectation that prayer could change or improve anything, either within me or my environment. Quite honestly I rarely wondered if there was anything in me that needed changing. Things were drifting along with surface calm. Then I developed an ulcer.

Outwardly the life to which I returned from World War II was ideal . . . the Redlands campus was as serene, my work as satisfying, my wife and small daughters as entrancing as ever. There was no obvious discord or strain. Yet, here I was with symptoms acknowledged to have their roots in personality adjustments.

Trained to recognize that symptoms in these cases must be by-passed to diagnose causes, I took a series of psychological tests which revealed that I was churning with the Big Four personality trouble-makers: Hate, Fear, Inferiority, Guilt. The accent in my case was on a form of hate known as disguised hostility. That the resulting ulcer was painful was undeniable. That I couldn't afford it was equally so. The accepted treatment was the analyst's couch at twenty-five dollars a visit. Obviously I couldn't support an analyst and a growing family. But I could not afford to let detrimental emotions play havoc with my peace of mind and physical body. It was apparent that I needed to rid myself of hostility. But how? To say, "Stop being hostile, all you need is love," I found on a par with saying, "Stop hurting, all you need is health," or "Don't worry, all you need is faith."

As a matter of fact, when you round up the opinions

of the experts and find that some demon, large or small, mars the daily life of almost our entire adult population, the question of how to rid oneself of any variation on the Big Four before real mental or physical damage is done becomes the million dollar question.

Today, clergymen, physicians, psychologists, psychiatrists know that few individuals are entirely free from mental turmoil, inner conflicts, increasing tensions, jarring human relationships. While bodily symptoms may not appear, it has been proved to everyone's satisfaction that fear and its cousins (hate and all rancor) strain the flow of normal health and block curative powers. Both serve to cloud the mind and a murky mind is a trouble-maker.

These intensified emotions do produce bodily disturbances. A famous physician, once professor of social ethics at Harvard Medical School, makes the statement that 75 per cent of the healing work of the physician could be done by the pastor. Young interns, the physicians of tomorrow, estimate that between 50 and 75 per cent of those who come for treatment have nothing organically wrong. Symptoms they can relieve. Permanent cure in the realm of psychosomatic medicine lies in the treatment of the whole man: body, mind and spirit.

Per capita the United States has more cases of extreme mental disorder than any other nation in the world. One out of every twenty Americans can expect to be in a mental institution during his lifetime. Admitting alcohol as an obsession of the mind, one family in five will have direct contact with mental unbalance.

In this picture, any therapy that can effect a better balance of our personality, which has a healing effect on the mind, will benefit the whole man. Therapy, in Webster's definition, is "that pertaining to the healing arts. Curative. Having healing qualities."

In my personal time of need I began to wonder if prayer, specifically applied, would fit that definition, would fulfill the promises made for it. I decided to try.

My first shock came when I found how little I knew about prayer. My second when I took a good look at my concept of God. What was I praying *to?* When I began I felt much like the little boy whose mother found him "drawing a picture of God."

"But, son," she protested. "Nobody knows what God looks like."

"Well," he said. "They will when I get finished."

I did not know what "picture" of God would emerge from my efforts. My first attempts at prayer were stumbling and groping. Yet, in three months I was a man with no ulcer and a new outlook on life. I couldn't rest there. This was proof for me as a man. As a scientist, I wanted to check the results, to explore and document techniques I had only glimpsed fleetingly in my personal experiment.

Thus, in 1951, at the University of Redlands we conducted the first controlled experiment satisfying academic conditions in prayer as a specific therapy or healing agent. It led to specific "hows." To specific methods of combining all knowledge available in the field. We found out how to make the journey from fear to faith; how to deal with hate, so damaging in every form, so far flung in our time; how to love our enemy, boss, in-laws, those who persecuted us; how inferiority gives place to adequacy and guilt to the acceptance of forgiveness, the honest evaluation and measure of each of us as a Son of Man and a Son of God.

A woman who entered the class when her husband, according to medical decree, had six months to live came to terms with death and then with life. Five years later her husband was still alive and well, and physicians were without explanation. So were the young couple. "But in a way we both died," the wife said. "To our old way of looking at things. You could say we were both 'born anew.' "

Did we find a way to immunize ourselves and our children against these destructive emotional forces? In a class of college students we found that prayer was the answer, that prayer therapy is a preventative as sure and effective as a vaccination against smallpox.

An ambitious young fraternity man, a football player

and campus leader, joined one student class because he frankly, and a little cynically, didn't want to miss any bets "if prayer has any provable power." He had his own opinions. "I knew it would lull and quiet a woman," he said later. "But would it accomplish anything concrete? I went to observe the laboratory effects on the others . . . the guinea pigs."

His surprise was enormous when the chief effects were on himself, when he learned what contacting this new and real Power did in re-forming his life. "To find this Power," he said, "coupled with free choice gives enormous hope and meaning to each individual existence."

Our work differed not only in our academic approach but in our emphasis. Church groups have been attempting to incorporate psychology and allied advances dealing with the personality. But so much emphasis has been put on the "ology," on group and private therapy, that conclusions in many instances led to a mistaken idea that the *power* lay in these types of therapy.

Our experiments proved the *power* lay with *God*.

No one in our classes was helped or healed by the power of the group, the application of psychology, nor by myself as the leader. The actual work was accomplished in the "homework" assigned between our single meetings each week. These meetings were for the purpose of studying and sharing. We discovered that prayer was a practice in honesty. Prayer was the bridge. But the healing power lay in a God of Love which each student found by "going into the closet and shutting the door."

When early reports of our experiment were published, results were incomplete. Still hundreds of people wrote, wired and called saying they wished to come immediately for instruction. It was with heavy hearts that we turned them away but this was never a part of our plan, nor a present possibility. Our work was investigating, testing, proving, and that work is growing and expanding. Presently other experiments based on ours are being undertaken at universities here and in England. Who knows what may happen, if as much careful, unprejudiced research goes into this science, with the greatest of all potentials, as has gone into the physical sciences? Who knows where we would be today if *spiritual research* had gone hand in hand with the other researches over two-thousand years?

But we know from over 10,000 letters, half of them from men, many from professionals, that the hunger for more light is acute. This is in no wise a textbook for classwork. It is not an academic book. It is the simple report on our work, a humble offer to share joyfully the light that was granted us, for here, indeed, is a "healing" art, a therapy adapted to every age, problem and condition.

And it is free to all!

William R. Parker
Redlands, California

PRAYER
CAN CHANGE
YOUR LIFE

1

EXPERIMENTS IN PRAYER

SEVERAL YEARS AGO, IN ONE OF THE FIRST OF THE "how to" series, the humorist, Will Cuppy, offered some interesting comments on "How to Become Extinct." "If the reader wishes to become extinct," Mr. Cuppy invited, "and is willing to take the trouble . . ." Most readers probably felt it would be no trouble at all. Since, according to Mr. Funk and Mr. Wagnall, to be extinct is to be "put out, quenched, hence inactive, disused, worn out," and eventually "extinguished or exterminated," the effort hardly seemed worth while.

However, day by day, hour by hour, year in and year out, a great many of us take a good deal of trouble and expend a considerable amount of fretful energy only to wind up "put out, inactive, worn out," and, in extreme cases, with sufficient effort, so handicapped that the life force is to all practical purposes "extinguished." We are useless, old before our time, worried, fearful, ill, or simply confused and not at all sure that this rat-race called life has a purpose. If any hope remains it is too apt to be for "tomorrow." If we think there is something ahead and are optimistic, we may look forward to heaven, again tomorrow, or some days or years after tomorrow, with or without stops along the way.

Obviously no one would deliberately walk toward extinction. Yet it is impossible to stand still. We are moving in some direction. If we are not experiencing a more abundant life from day to day we may be sure we are traveling away from life. It is equally certain that, unless we radically change our direction today, we cannot look forward to suddenly making the grade the further side of eternity. It is now, today, or never.

This conviction has appeared consistently in one form or another among thoughtful men right down the ages. The Apostle Paul insisted that "Now is the day of salvation." More recently the great sculptor, Auguste Rodin, said plaintively, "I do not understand why we demand another life, since we have not learned to enjoy and understand this one fully." Blaise Pascal put it with great clarity, "Always looking forward to being happy, it is inevitable that we should never be so." According to them, the fullness of life is something we can begin to find today!

Then the all important question is, how? How do we change our direction and walk in serenity, physical well-being with sound mind and purpose, toward more abundant life? How do we begin to fully understand and enjoy day to day existence?

Men in all fields, sensing the urgent need for answers, have been doing their level best. Clergymen, metaphysicians, psychiatrists, psychologists, and in their wake hypnotists, cultists, astrologists, spiritualists, all sincere, extend their theories and promises. "Follow me!" "Try me!" "Eat me . . . drink me . . ." until the bewildered seeker feels a bit like Alice in Wonderland nibbling first at this and then at that, adding theory to theory, confusion on confusion, until the last state of the man may be worse than the first.

You've Got to Show Me!

Since this book will give some definite answers to those questions, since these answers are based on scientific, accurate, measurable experiments, the first step is to show why we can make bold, life-saving claims for the power of prayer as it unfolded to us in a nine-

month experiment conducted at the University of Redlands.

A retired banker who had heard of our work and was
interested in joining a subsequent Prayer Therapy class,
asked me for an interview. He had been talking to a member of the original experimental Prayer Therapy Group
who promised him that our techniques in prayer, plus a
Key provided by psychology, would "heal his diseases,
renew his mind and body, calm the storms of daily living." In short, it would lead him to a kingdom of abundant life, of peace that passeth understanding, here and
now. He had need of all these things. Outwardly, materially, this need was not apparent. Dignified, self-con-
trolled, a man of parts so-called, he appeared to be everything that we call a success. Yet his wife was on the
verge of leaving him, his relationships with his only son
were heart-breaking, his accumulated wealth seemed
pointless and the years spent acquiring it wasted years.

His tragedy, like that of so many of us, was not that
he was close to a hospital or insane asylum, but as a normal, intelligent man, he was leading a life of "quiet desperation." The more he searched and the harder he
sought answers, the more disappointed he became and
questioned any new solution. This banker fellow, while
clinging doggedly to a faith in the principle he called
God, had acquired a sound, businesslike skepticism regarding different approaches to Him.

"Do you remember," he asked, sitting quietly in my
office during our interview, "a speech made by a con-
gressman half a century ago before a Naval Banquet in
Philadelphia? He said, 'I come from a state that raises
corn and cotton and cockleburs . . . Frothy eloquence
neither convinces nor satisfies me. I am from Missouri.
You have got to show me.'"

No one, he added, remembers today whether Con-
gressman William Duncan Vandiver referred to a money-
making machine, a patent medicine, or a new philosophy.
"And I'm from Arizona," he said. "However, I've tried
the money-making machine, several patent medicines and
a couple of new philosophies. I've earnestly sought help

through prayer. And I've had psychiatrists. I'm not much further along. The friend who sent me here says I've probably been 'praying amiss.' What makes him think so? He says psychiatry does not go far enough. How does he know? He thinks Prayer Therapy is my answer. You've either got a revolutionary proposition that deserves my full attention, or you've just added to the world's overflowing cup of 'frothy eloquence.' Well, I'm open-minded. But you've got to show me!"

Far from being upset, my personal feeling was that this was the only healthy approach. I hope you, reading these pages, will have the same one. It is the exact spirit in which the original experiment was conducted.

For myself, I had had a personal experience, a personal healing so effective and so moving that I had been "shown." I could not doubt the reality of the Power that had come to my aid or the method that had unfolded before my hesitant, fumbling efforts, but could it be repeated? Could it be proved? Was it based on a principle?

I am a college man myself, an academically trained animal. Even in the realm of religion and prayer, so long held in superstitious isolation from being subject to proof, I know that honest seekers in forty-seven states beside Missouri are recalling the words of James: "Faith without *works* is dead." The definite statement of the Master Christian Himself that "these *signs* shall follow them that believe . . ." the ability to cast out devils, to heal the sick.

A prominent west-coast newspaperwoman, walking in New York one day recently, chanced to see engraved on the cornerstone of a fashionable church the instructions Jesus gave to His followers: "Heal the sick, cleanse the lepers, raise the dead, cast out devils" (Matt. 10:8). On an impulse, she walked around to the rectory door and asked to see the rector.

"I saw your sign," she said. "Do you?"

"Sign?" asked the bewildered man. "Do I?"

"Do you 'heal the sick, cleanse the lepers, raise the dead, cast out devils'? If you don't, you shouldn't advertise it."

She did not mean it as a witticism or rebuke. It was

an earnest question as to whether these "signs" were indeed following a man who believed. We had once discussed together, this friend and I, the statement that 75 per cent of the healing work of the physician could be done by the pastor. Because she believed that, because she wanted to believe it, she was issuing a challenge. A longing for something solid to believe in, and an inability to accept empty promises, that is the temper of the times. In that temper, when a new concept is offered, the reaction is immediate. "Prove to me that it is worth my while to investigate this. If you can do this, then tell me simply, without froth or eloquence, what your technique is and how I may use it."

This is a straightforward, honest proposition. It calls for a straightforward, honest answer to these points, exactly as they are stated. And so it is my plan, in this book, to offer first a proof that Prayer Therapy has changed lives, has worked on principle, and what our experiments indicated was *wrong* with prayer as most of us have habitually practiced it, as well as what is *missing* from psychology without prayer.

These questions answered, you, the seeker, can bring an open mind and an honest trust and willingness to the simple explanation which follows of exactly what Prayer Therapy is and how it can be used in individual life.

The "Guinea Pigs"

If the Prayer Experiment begun at the University of Redlands in September, 1951, was to prove anything at all, it had to have measurable results. Thus the human guinea pigs who participated were, by and large, "the lame, the halt and the blind," a cross section of ordinary humanity suffering in some degree discords of mind and body. The more exaggerated the condition, the more obvious would be those results. The entire group was limited to forty-five volunteers, two-thirds purposely not from the University itself but from surrounding cities and towns. They were housewives, foundry workers, ranchers, ultra-smart society women, teachers, businessmen, a minister, an artist . . . rich, poor, as young as twenty-two, as old as sixty. They came recommended by physicians, clergymen, friends, or simply because they had heard of the proposed experiment and were interested in joining it.

It must be clear that not one, the minister excepted (this failure to make his theology "work" will be dealt with later), was a theologian, a philosopher, or a student of psychology. They were not interested in a discussion group, in old dogma or new theory. Their common bond was that each had a definite need to be met and was willing to seek a solution with an open mind. They wanted results!

True, some already believed their remedy was at hand in prayer. Others tended toward psychotherapy. There were those, too, who did not know what to believe or even if there was anything to believe in. What they did know positively was that they were traveling in the direction of being "inactive, worn out" and even "extinguished." Some had only exaggerated fears, lengthened shadows of the worry and depression which dogs us all from time to time. Others belonged to that 50 to 75 per cent who seek medical treatment when there is nothing organically wrong. This is not to be confused with hypochondria. Genuine symptoms exist and genuine pain, but their nature is psychosomatic. Since psychosomatic merely means a physical disorder induced by emotional factors, it was obvious why medical treatment could only relieve these symptoms. No recommendation was made, therefore, for or against continued medical treatment during the experiment. Since the admitted cause lay within the individual, in his personality adjustment, obviously the cure would have to be wrought there and medical treatment would have no bearing on the accuracy of our results. Not only would it be humane to let the individual be as comfortable as possible, but it was our purpose to use *all* the wisdom and help that has been granted us.

Obviously, whether they were suffering visible psychomatic symptoms, which include migraine headache, arthritis, tuberculosis, functional heart trouble, high blood pressure, acne, allergies, or were simply fast becoming nervous wrecks, these forty-five individuals were moving farther and farther away from that "victorious life" which some unquenchable inner instinct keeps assuring man is his birthright.

Here was appropriate raw material upon which to test the power of Christian prayer. Among the multitudes that followed the Nazarene carpenter, Jesus, who established the principles of that power, were always those crying for bodily healing, for casting out of the devils that tormented them. And He healed them, cast out their devils, then promised "those who believed" that they could do likewise. Was that an idle promise? Could proof that it was a present possibility be established today? These were the questions we had to answer.

2

MEASURING PRAYER POWER

IF THE AVERAGE MAN HAS FINALLY REACHED A POINT where he is saying flatly, "You have got to show me," the academic world is even more definite. For any experiment to be of real service at the scientific level, it must meet the demands for comparison as well as measurable results.

The point of comparison was a challenging one. Each in his separate field, the clergyman with religion, the academic expert with psychology, the medically trained with psychiatry, had been trying to free man from the increasing mental turmoil, those inner conflicts and tensions, those jarring human relationships that lead to much of the evil that besets us.

Each field could claim victories and failures, progress and setbacks. But walls of misunderstanding, of precedent and procedure, the zealous guarding of professional boundaries, seemed to prohibit their joining hands to solve the common problem.

It was rather like the situation Will Rogers found in Washington during the bleakest years of the depression. Everywhere he encountered debates, plans, schemes, activity, but he saw little hope for the relief of "the fellow who is hungry now." Will said, "I don't think we have anybody in Washington that don't want to feed 'em, but they all want to feed 'em their way."

Since the Prayer Therapy Group would attempt to combine the highest unfoldment in all fields at the university level where it would be free to blend and experiment without fear of trespassing the rights of each of those unwritten barriers that limit the effective use of all, it would be under careful scrutiny.

While forward-looking physicians, clergymen, psychologists recommended individuals for the experiment, there were reactionaries who sat back and waited. Some clergymen questioned the need for psychological aid in prayer when confession was open to all. A few psychologists and psychiatrists, justifiably proud of the advancement of their clinical procedures, questioned the purpose or benefit in trying to add religion.

These questions had to be answered.

Supposing favorable results were noted from the use of Prayer Therapy (prayer, rightly understood and practiced, plus psychology). Who, in all honesty, could say whether the use of psychotherapy alone, without any prayer, might not have obtained even better results? Or that the habitual prayer of the devout individual, without any assist from psychology or new techniques, might not have effected a quicker and more complete adjustment to the problem?

As the academic corner would phrase it: Was it clinically possible to prove first, the efficacy of Prayer Therapy, and then (assuming it proved effective), compare its merits relative to Just-Plain-Prayer and Just-Plain-Psychology?

Laboratory techniques with rats, mice and genuine guinea pigs are fairly common knowledge among laymen today. If a scientist wishes to establish the relative merit of a diet of grain-plus-vitamins against just-plain-grain, one group of guinea pigs called a control group is relentlessly kept to a diet of just-plain-grain during the time the other group is receiving the fortified food and the results are fearlessly observed and tabulated. Obviously an experiment in Prayer Therapy can be no less thorough and fearless and must include control groups.

The Control Groups

For this purpose the forty-five volunteers were interviewed and carefully divided into three equal groups of fifteen individuals each. This number seemed to us large enough to indicate a strong trend, and still small enough to handle effectively.

        Group   I—15—Psychotherapy
        Group   II—15—Random Pray*ers*
        Group III—15—Prayer Therapy

Group I was offered the best psychology could provide in weekly individual counseling to bring to light and remove emotional disorders. No mention of religion was made and the fifteen selected for this category either expressed a definite preference for psychotherapy or had been specifically recommended for this type of treatment by their physician. This control group would represent Just-Plain-Psychology.

Group II were all schooled in a theological denomination and were faithful, practicing Christians. Each expressed a confidence in prayer as a definite solution to his or her emotional and physical ills, believed psychology an unnecessary adjunct, and felt that they already knew how to pray. This they agreed to do every night before retiring for the duration of the experiment, the nine months of the college semester year, using their present concept of prayer with the specific objective of overcoming the problem at hand. No psychological insight into what inharmonies within them needed prayer help was offered and no techniques in prayer suggested. These fifteen, whom we called the Random Pray*ers,* represented the Just-Plain-Prayer control group.

Group III became the first Prayer Therapy Group, meeting weekly for a two hour session in the converted Army barracks which normally serves as the University Speech Clinic. Some of the class which found its way faithfully to the improvised laboratory hidden in a clump of oak trees between the back door of the imposing administration building and the University Park made a sixty mile drive from Los Angeles and one regular came from Long Beach, seventy-two miles to the south. Here amid the building blocks, the wooden hammer and musical instruments used by children in play therapy, fifteen earnest, excited adults began the first investigation in prayer ever to submit itself and its result to the rigid requirements of the academic searchlight.

The separate groups had no connection or communication with each other and only myself, my assistants, and the outside psychologist who administered tests were aware of just how close the comparisons would be in certain cases.

There were, for instance, three women, one in each group, whose physicians had told them they faced nervous breakdowns.

Mabel McN. was an attractive woman of thirty-three with a better-than-average education. She was married to a successful real estate man and was the mother of two sons. Following the death of her mother-in-law some years previous, Mabel, who had hated the older woman with a fervent fury, succumbed to a breakdown. Recently she had been under medical treatment for anemia and a painful back condition. When Dr. Y., failing to find the cause of the back difficulty, had a long talk with Mabel, he felt that most of her difficulty was emotional and recommended her to us for personal counseling.

When I first talked with her the prayer experiment was forming and she was interested. She didn't think much of prayer, however, and had "tried praying but did not feel helped," although she had been raised in a religious atmosphere, sent her sons to Sunday School, and "supposed she believed in God." Since she had come for psychotherapy and wanted it, she was placed in Group I, the Just-Plain-Psychology control group.

Esther W., on the other hand, was confident that prayer, her own type of prayer, would give her the help she needed. Esther had heard a talk at a local Protestant church in which the proposed experiment at the University was described and she immediately volunteered for the Just-Plain-Prayer group. Deeply devout, Esther, at thirty-two, had always attended church regularly and since her health had been bad, attended almost constantly. Married, with two children, she was the graduate of a large mid-western university, an accomplished musician and had been teaching the fifth grade in public school for some time.

She was aware of her need for Divine help, Esther said. Following a physical examination a month before, the doctor could find no organic cause for her exaggerated nervous condition, for her loss of physical energy, her depression. She "couldn't stand" her household, "couldn't stand" her school class, just "couldn't stand" anything in her daily life. Her physician told her he could give her something to quiet her nerves, but assured her that, unless she received mental and emotional help, a nervous breakdown could follow.

At the time of that first interview, Esther felt that the presence in her home of a divorced sister-in-law was the chief contributing factor to her condition, that God alone could get her out of the house, and that "prayer can give me the only possible mental and emotional help." So she agreed to pray regularly each night at home with the answer to her specific need as her objective.

The Prayer Therapy class in no instance got the easiest of the cases.

Mrs. V. was already a three-time loser, had suffered nervous breakdowns at eighteen, at twenty-six, and again at thirty-eight. Now, at fifty-three, her physician felt that she was not far from a fourth. A wealthy woman of the world, a social leader, graduate of a famous eastern women's college, Mrs. V. had to admit something was amiss. She had been married almost thirty years, two of her three grown children were married, and her readjustment to the new life and role of mother-in-law seemed to try her beyond her resources. That she felt her condition was serious was evidenced by the fact that she, who was far from an individualist, far from confident in doing things nobody else did, was willing to join hands with the fourteen other guinea pigs and arrive openly at the Army barracks each week.

I confessed my surprise when she asked to join and remarked that it was urgent with us that those who entered the project remained to the end. She smiled and said, "Dr. Parker, I've been everywhere. I've tried everything . . . and I must find help. Maybe I don't look it but I'm . . . well, I'm desperate."

The similarity between Mrs. V., Mabel and Esther, from the obvious point of view, was about the same as the similarity between tweeds, glazed chintz and alligator with mink. But as case histories, they had a deep similarity and we were to watch the outcome with real interest. In the end, the progress of Mabel McN. was to illustrate one facet of our experiment more clearly than any other single case we encountered.

Of equal interest from the point of comparison were three "ineffectual" men who entered the project, each in a different group.

Bart appeared to be a well placed white-collar man, employed in a bank, with a pretty white-collar wife and three healthy children. On the advice of his physician, who simply could not locate reasonable causes for the long array of complaints that took Bart to his clinic each week, he advised him to seek help with us through psychotherapy.

When he first came for an interview, Bart had a defiant manner and a hatful of accusations against life in general. He was always, he said, by-passed at the bank when it came time for promotion. His fellow employees were no better than they should be. His attitude toward them was one of a superiority he did not truly feel and their response was to make him fully realize his unpopularity.

At home Bart was what is commonly called a worm, a man of a totally different nature. Far from assuming any superiority, he did dishes, pushed a vacuum cleaner, sulked because his children ran all over him. He was not the man of the house at home. He was not secure at the bank. "My business life's a mess," he said. "And my home life's worse." At the age of forty-one, he felt quite simply that, if this was all there was to it, he did not want any more. The mention of Prayer Therapy brought out the fact that he had received so much compulsory theological training in his youth that he was openly antagonistic, if not atheistic, but he would be glad to be a case history in the experiment's Just-Plain-Psychology group. "The others are for crackpots anyhow," he announced, "and nobody will get a thing out of 'em."

That remained to be seen. Certainly it was visible to the naked eye that this man was ineffectual and there was room for help. It was not so, however, with Jerry S. Except for a kind of perpetual frown, Jerry was a good-looking, red-headed lad of twenty-two, the only son of a Protestant minister, and didn't look ineffectual at all.

Yet he had failed to finish college, could not stick to one job, was depressed, nervous and subject to headaches which seemed to have no organic cause. But the real tragedy Jerry unfolded was his conviction that he was a misfit. He could not relate himself to others and felt his human relationships were unbearable. He spent a tremendous amount of time quarreling violently with his parents upon whom he nevertheless continued to depend. It was his father who, in desperation, had persuaded him to talk to me.

The talk revealed that Jerry had a great desperation of his own. He had no belief in the future, no belief in life, there was no purpose or point that he could see. He was, and knew he was, ineffectual, and this made him fighting mad.

"Your deepest need, I think," I told him, "is to find yourself, what you really are, and your place in God's scheme of things." With this he agreed. But when I mentioned psychotherapy as a means of finding himself, he announced that he didn't "believe in Freud and those old birds." Nor was he interested in the Prayer Therapy Group because, as he said, "I know about God and I honestly believe in Him and I've been raised on prayer all my life." But he wanted very much, he said, to be a part of the Random Prayer group. "I've never prayed specifically on my problem," he said, "but I know if I do, it'll be answered. Being part of the experiment will help me to do it faithfully each night."

The last of the trio of ineffectual men, the one who joined the Prayer Therapy students, was himself a Protestant minister. Sixty years old, married with three grown daughters, Reverend G. held a doctor's degree and was intellectually brilliant. Yet he had spent his entire life playing second fiddle, first to one pastor then another, never at any time being offered a church of his own. Nor could he win any confidence, friendship and love from the members of the congregation. "I am," he said, "a failure, and I know it." His doctor's degree did him more harm than good for, obviously, his assumed intellectual superiority separated him from others and left him isolated and lonely. Although he was a splendidly built, robust man, his personality cast an aura of condescension like a cloud around him, his manner of speaking was critical and exacting, while his inner frustrations and tensions resulted in a nervous tic and a revolting habit of constantly clicking his teeth.

Rev. G. particularly requested admission to the Prayer Therapy group. "I'd like to join your investigation. I have been praying for many years," he said. "There must be either more to prayer than I know about, or much less than I've always hoped."

I was to remember those revealing words later when he had begun specific work in the Prayer Therapy class, but at the beginning I was simply content to welcome such an interesting guinea pig, and academically interested that, once more, despite surface differences in age, symptoms and circumstances, these three ineffectual men were suffering, in common, excessive frustration and loneliness and demonstrating thoroughly unsuccessful lives. But each case had to be subjected to a different form of treatment.

Klaus had no counterpart, in any other group. He was unique and, on the other hand, I think the single biggest challenge ever brought for solution by Prayer Therapy. For Klaus was "hopeless." Medicine said so. Psychiatry said so. Religion said so, or rather Klaus told religion so, for he was an atheist. Both desperately ill and a "sinner," in many senses, Klaus was the man nobody wanted.

He was only thirty-seven when he asked to join the experimental Prayer Therapy Group. "I've heard about it and, well, it is about my last hope. I've got to try something. They say I'm past medical help." A talented sketch artist with artistic training, he was then working in a pottery plant, "but I never know how long I'm going to be working anywhere." Klaus was at that time subject to as many as six epileptic fits a day of the Grand Mal type, which are the most serious of all. From 1935-1936 he had been a patient at Craig Colony, New York. More recently he had been hospitalized in a county institution under medical and psychiatric care for palsy, once for a nervous breakdown, twice for alcoholism. For years he had been under heavy sedation. Although he was married and had a small daughter, Klaus readily admitted that he had also undergone a cure for venereal disease.

This man's background was a nightmare of heartbreak and frustration. An orphan who never knew who his parents were, he had lived for a time with a family that was no-better-than-it-should-be. When they were hustled off to jail just before Klaus completed the ninth grade, the youngster was left completely on his own. It was obvious at thirty-seven that his own hadn't been good enough. Aside from his physical defects, he and his wife had sexual problems and lived under explosive tensions unbelievable to the average person.

Klaus, when he entered our group, held a full house in the game of human evils—a marital problem, a financial problem, mental, moral and psychical difficulties. Here was a prize guinea pig for any impartial experiment and, as a scientist, I welcomed him. As a human being, my sympathy went out to him for, despite his obvious shortcomings, his bitterness and disillusion, Klaus' eyes sparked with a native intelligence, his humor was shy but quick, even his ridiculous black mustache made him look more like Charlie Chaplin's tramp when nobody came to dinner than like the dapper being Klaus imagined it turned him into. And Klaus' suffering was so intense that he was stripped of all smugness. He, at least, was not comfortable in his sins.

This, of course, did not end the list of individual cases, but they serve best to illustrate the comparative point. There were others, ulcer sufferers in two groups, arthritics and asthmatics, victims of migraine headache, that blinding onslaught that comes from nowhere and reduces a strong man to complete uselessness for the duration.

In later chapters these and other stories will be shared with the reader to clarify specific "hows." But those selected here were outstanding from the point of viewing the relative merits of the leading techniques currently accepted for help. This important aspect covered, we were faced with the second requirement for an academic experiment, measurable results.

The Scientific Yardstick and Its Uses

Psychology provided us with our yardstick for measuring results . . . five generally accepted tests scientifically designed to probe the subconscious and unveil the detrimental aspects within the personality make-up. These tests were given privately off-campus to each individual in the entire experiment at the *beginning* and the *end* of the project by a skilled psychometrist with a degree in psychology who was in no way involved directly in the work we were doing.

These tests included the Rorschach, commonly called the "ink-blot" test. It is literally a series of specially designed ink blots on ten separate cards. By the imaginative responses a person gives it reveals something about his personality. It reveals some of the inner dynamics of personality. It does not rely on "logical" answers that most paper and pencil tests represent. Intellectual capacity as well as functional impairment of capacity, cerebral damage and the nature of the illness may be rather accurately charted by the Rorschach. It should be given only by a highly trained and competent tester.

The Szondi Test utilizes pictures of mental patients with a known disease and is based on the hypothesis that "like attracts like." Choice patterns rather than projective elaboration determine the record. Clinical use of the test indicates that the patterns of choice are characteristic of certain personality syndromes.

The Thematic Apperception Test is commonly referred to as the TAT. A number of pictures are used to stimulate fantasy that vary from the type found in magazine illustrations with human figures to abstract and vague representations. The photographs and drawings allow for the free expression of inner attitudes and feelings. The TAT often helps to pinpoint the defenses that were merely suggested by the Rorschach.

Two familiar tests are the Sentence Completion and Word Association Tests. A part of a sentence is shown or read to the person which they are to complete with the first thought that comes to their mind. This may be quite revealing. This is the Sentence Completion Test. In the Word Association Test a series of clinically designed words are given orally to the subject, one at a time, and the subject is to respond to each word with the first word that occurs to him. The subject is told that it does not matter what his response is, but that it should be the first word that comes to his mind after he hears the word the tester calls out. The reaction time, the response given, and observations of behavior are all taken into account.

On the final test at the conclusion of the experiment, these would indicate to a trained observer the elimination or improvement or backsliding (regression) of any specific emotional difficulty just as surely as Junior's math exam charted his mastery of that subject.

Symptomatic improvement would, of course, be obvious. Personal interviews would be interesting and helpful in analyzing techniques. But for academic measuring purposes, these accepted tests would be the best possible basis for evaluating the individual's success or failure to progress under a given technique.

They would also serve as a basis for a prognosis, an expert prediction at the beginning of the improvement possible to the individual after a sort of worm's-eye-view of what material lay beneath the surface, in the subconscious.

The results and prognosis were not, of course, shown to the person involved. They would, however, serve as guides for the individual counselor in the psychotherapy group. Also, they were the basis for the Key which would be used in Prayer Therapy. Since this Key was a most important factor in our Prayer Therapy work we need to look now at the "why" and "how" of it. The "why" was obvious.

While some clergymen questioned the need for this psychological aid when confession was available, it had been my personal experience that I myself was unaware of the very things that had caused my ulcer. The examination of conscience as practiced by most of us dwells chiefly on "sin," the sins of omission and commission. "I lied . . . I cheated . . . I stole . . . I lost my temper . . . I failed to . . ." Normal guilt, thus recognized, is a spur to new patterns needed for a healthy soul. But things causing the greatest pain, the deepest shame, "I fear . . . and what I fear . . . I hate . . . and whom and what I hate . . ." the emotional "sins" are shoved out of conscious sight into the subconscious, there to fester in darkness, the root of most of our personal evils. The very thoughts of "sin" and condemnation act as a sentinel between conscious knowing and subconscious burying.

The "how" of bringing these things to the individual Prayer Therapy student's conscious mind was carefully worked out before the project began by myself and the graduate assistants who helped me. We decided to pass out to each member every week a sealed envelope containing a slip of paper on which was written one detrimental personality aspect as revealed by the individual's tests.

Beside the off-campus psychologist who administered them, only I and my assistants saw the completed results and prognosis from the series of tests. We used these to select the undesirable emotion which was to be given the student on his "slip." His homework, then, was the elimination or improvement of this specific aspect by prayer, a definite type of prayer.

The envelopes were handed out at the conclusion of each session and each envelope was sealed to ensure personal privacy. No public soul-baring was suggested by us. However, as the experiment progressed and the participants found no condemnation in their fellow classmates, they voluntarily began discussing the content of their private slips and sharing their own experiences and progress reports in dealing with their difficulties. Inhibitions and barriers crumbled as they recognized that each of them needed help and healing, and that each had something to share with the other, if it was only encouragement. Throughout the experiment, however, we adhered to the policy of the sealed envelope, leaving it to the individual to bring its content into class discussion.

From this innovation provided by psychology we developed the more detailed Key offered in Chapter 4, and the new methods for evaluating oneself, the modern examination of conscience as it unfolded to the Prayer Therapy Group, charted specifically for the reader's use in Chapters 11 and 12.

What the Tests Revealed

Sharing with the reader the results of some of these early tests it will be easier to see the common denominator underlying similar symptoms.

In the case of Mabel McN., the attractive thirty-three-year-old mother who had suffered a nervous breakdown following the death of her mother-in-law, and whose physician sent her for personal counseling, believing her to be verging on another breakdown, she was rigid in her desire to conform.

In her verbal conversation with the tester, she kept insisting that "everything was just lovely," because so such things should be, and then blaming everyone around her, including her dead mother-in-law, for every annoying situation which she refused to face in her "just-

lovely" world. The need to hold everything and everyone around her to a rigid pattern, coupled with the inability to face or come to terms with reality, meant two
unreal worlds . . . the "just-lovely-world" into which
others wouldn't conform and her own private fantasy-
land into which she escaped when she could not bear
the hodge-podge around her or did not wish to make a
decision.

Her basic difficulty was that she had no strong belief
in anything to hold onto. She didn't feel capable of loving anyone, least of all herself and figured "there is something lacking in me." She was afraid of her own thoughts,
and anxiety, depression and tension were the obvious
results of trying to fit everything into unreality.

The prognosis in her instance was good and the tester
felt if she could be "helped to accept (love) herself as
she really is, she will be on the road to recovery."

Esther W., the devout thirty-two-year-old schoolteacher in the Random Prayer Group, also facing a nervous breakdown, was likewise rigid in her desire to conform, yet explained her reasons for refusing to face reality
or make decisions because "the world was wicked anyhow and what's the use?" She definitely did not expect
any good thing *now* but looked for it in a possible kingdom *later,* which served her as a logical reason for turning
her back on her problems or trying to solve them and
gave her her own personal kind of fantasy-land.

Esther's feelings of insecurity were strong and her desire to escape both notice and personal decisions led to
her rigid attempt to make her life and everyone else's
conform exactly to outward formal patterns. Again, she
blamed the lack of "fitting into" this pattern on her sister-
in-law, her husband, her students, almost anyone else
and her personal relations were most unhappy. Her physical relations with her husband were tortuous to her, for
there was neither relaxation nor acceptance in her attitude, and the marriage ceremony itself had terrified her.
In view of the results of her nine months of prayer, it is
important to note here that her father, while deeply religious, had been exacting, critical and harsh in adminis-

tering justice and she had experienced little praise or encouragement from him. The prognosis was positive.

Mrs. V., the fifty-three-year-old social leader with three breakdowns to her credit already and confronting a fourth, destined for the Prayer Therapy experimental group, was the most tragically mixed up of the trio.

Here the tests revealed a woman basically endowed with exceptional gifts, mentally and spiritually, while also possessing everything of a material nature that the heart could wish. Yet all the material goods benefited her little, while the invisible gifts were repressed, rigidly held down by a program of conforming to obvious and outward sterile social customs. She would accept anyone's pattern, however inferior, to her own. She could not trust herself, her judgment nor impulses, but held all things stiffly to Emily Post or the "old school tie" or some code, including her children, her sex life, her position as a mother-in-law, or her relationship with others. Tortured as a mother-in-law, a wife, a friend, she was never quite sure she did the "right thing" in the eyes of others; her fear of her own inadequacy kept her from even daring to evaluate what the right thing was in her own eyes. Like putting kittens in a basket, every time she felt she had everything neatly under control, something or someone popped out of line and she felt furiously that they were "at fault." This Emily Post world was her escape, her fantasy-land, but so much fear, so much inadequacy, so much repression and insecurity had developed in her a thriving hostility buried firmly below the polite level of self-recognition, yet smoldering always beneath that rigid control like a volcano forever in danger of breaking forth.

Her prognosis was excellent if anything could persuade her to abandon an imitation of life for the actual business of living it. Common to all three of these women was a rigid desire to conform, a tendency to blame others, the inability to make decisions or face the world as it really existed for them.

Of the three "ineffectual men," the first two (Bart in Personal Counseling, and Jerry, the minister's young son in Random Prayer) showed a decided will to failure. This Will to Fail is more common than most of us would believe and extremely easy to fall into because in odd ways, there is a certain amount of success guaranteed the man who wills to fail. It takes effort, but almost anyone can do it.

One of the chief rewards for not trying is that, while you never know how high you might have climbed, you are never, never forced to face your limitations. There is always that "might have been." "If I had *really* tried, I could have done better." And, so long as you don't *really* try, there is no one to deny it.

Of course, the other guy gets paid for it, has the success of it, but the individual with the Will to Fail still has his ego complete. Those who protect themselves with the rewards of failure (the drinker, the dreamer, the sleeper, who refuse to live more than twelve hours and must dream away the other twelve in unconscious activity, actually dream activity, the pathological reader, the "bone lazy" specimen) are moving away from living life and succeeding at it as quickly as their will to fail will permit them. They truly move toward extinction whether they know it or not.

Hence, to find both Bart and Jerry, the ineffectuals, sharing a will to fail was not surprising. Jerry's failure had produced an unusual amount of success for him. If he failed at college, at one job after another, lost friends or girl friends in rapid sequence, the true causes were never faced by either Jerry or his parents. In misguided love and with great injustice, all such things were rationalized comfortably away, Jerry was comforted and some delightful new thing was found for Jerry to do. Jerry remained emotionally immature. Naturally, with many invented reasons, Jerry kept on failing, spared forever the necessity of control or effort that makes for a real try for success and the deep shame of missing the mark should an honest endeavor fail. Like Bart, the ineffectual bank employee and husband, Jerry kidded himself that "if he wanted to," "if other people were different," or "my family would let me alone" he could do all manner of wonderful things. This type of fairy tale did not assist Bart's emotional growth toward maturity either.

Both these men were overly dependent, anticipated trouble, yet below the surface, buried in the subconscious, was deep hostility and great guilt that neither was succeeding as a man.

Bart, nineteen years older than Jerry, stated that he "could have taken his household in hand if he wanted to play the heavy father." He could go on rationalizing and excusing himself thus and never risk discovering it might be a lie. It saved him a lot of trouble too. He also believed he could have "gotten ahead at the bank if I wanted to apple-polish like the rest of them." With such plausible rationalization, he needn't make any attempt and could continue in his fantasy world to believe this was true. One task of personal counseling would be to uncover for him this well-hidden will to fail.

With both Bart and Jerry there was more risk in succeeding, more chance of responsibility than an overly dependent man would care for. In both, self-doubt was strong, humiliation a deep fear, self-confidence the desired end. For both the prognosis was favorable, if they could develop a positive approach, based on the confidence that they could succeed through self-realization.

With the ineffectual Rev. G. in the Prayer Therapy group, the Will to Fail was born of a complex deeply hidden from his conscious knowledge. Here was a minister who was *afraid of God*. It was no wonder that his subconscious desire was to fail to convince anyone of salvation through Christ which he had preached for over thirty years. *He did not believe in it himself!*

The minister's case was the tragedy of high intellectual attainment coupled with a total lack of emotional belief or conviction, once again a form of emotional retarded growth, immaturity, "the letter without the spirit" laying waste his life. He was tormented with the fears and guilts which will attend any man who teaches, preaches or sells something which he either does not understand, or does not believe. There is a strong price to be paid in internal disorder where there is a betrayal of integrity, even though it is buried beyond conscious knowing. The Rev. G. had selected a respectable, profitable profession, used a brilliant mind to study every ramification of it, and wound up a failure, knowing little about life.

Here was the reverse of the story of the Cure of Ars who was once criticized as a totally uneducated man. "I don't know whether he is educated or not," remarked his Bishop, "but what I do know is that the Holy Ghost makes a point of enlightening him."

Rev. G. was highly educated but spiritually unenlightened and this made for a confused, unhappy, helpless minister, for formal education has never been a necessary ingredient for faith. It was easy to see that there was much underlying his spoken desire to join our Prayer Therapy experimental group, for there was, indeed, "either much more to prayer than he knew about . . . or much less than he had always *hoped*."

He had other difficulties as well. From his point of intellectual superiority he was not aware of people and their needs. He felt he must control every situation as he could do everything better than anyone else, hence he would not delegate authority. The tremendous conflict between his need for full control and his inability to handle people well brought on a real frustration. He wanted social and intellectual distances kept, yet now, after thirty years of playing second fiddle to one pastor after another, he had to admit he was a lonely man, a failure.

All this was so far from the conscious awareness of the reverend gentleman, who in many ways remained entirely satisfied with himself, that his prognosis was only fair while, in the case of Klaus, Prayer Therapy's guinea pig who appeared possessed of the Biblical seven devils, the prognosis, despite the failure of psychiatry and medicine to effect a previous cure, was excellent. The difference lay in the fact that Klaus was in no wise satisfied with Klaus.

Natively intelligent, rather than intellectual, Klaus made an amazing statement to the tester during his first interview. "I'd really like to find out what I have to work with, even if it hurts, so I can discard the rubbish and live a life that has purpose and direction and some degree of fulfillment of both the inner and outer man."

His tests revealed that what he had to work with was thoroughly jumbled to the point where even the acceptance of God as a possibility seemed beyond him. Yet this was the only form of therapy he hadn't tried . . . and try it he would . . . though God and evolution simply would not go together in his personal scheme of things.

Klaus' tests revealed him to be as full of bitterness, resentments and hostility as his small stature could hold. His early life had much to do with it, but beyond that, there were tremendous defiance and aggressions, and since it was imposible to turn these outward, he turned them in upon himself and there were spontaneous outbursts, epileptic fits, when the pressure became too much for his feeble control.

Toward sex he felt guilt and fear and his wife suffered as well as himself. Guilt, fear and anxiety dogged him in his relations with others, and that constant gnawing terror of a seizure when people stared and thought him crazy or drunk, when he could lose a job in the twinkling of an eye, or a new-made friend, or an old one; this specter had walked with Klaus for years. Thus, despite his artistic talent, his fine intelligence, Klaus constantly sabotaged his own efforts and ability through fear of failure, fear of being condemned and judged, fear of the censure of those among whom he lived.

The other sciences had failed. Klaus did not believe in God, nor the power of prayer. Could Prayer Therapy help him? It was the supreme challenge.

Here, then, were our guinea pigs: Klaus, Rev. G., Jerry, Bart, Mrs. V., Esther, Mabel, and thirty-eight others. The control groups were established, the results from the first tests were in. Group One began reporting regularly for weekly individual personal counseling. Group Two went off to pray faithfully each night. Group

Three commenced their regular weekly meetings in the Army barracks.

In nine months, for the first time in history, the results of a controlled experiment in prayer would be scientifically measured, compared and evaluated.

3

EXAMINING RESULTS

BY JUNE 18, 1952, EXACTLY NINE MONTHS AND TEN days after the experiment began, the final set of psychological tests for the forty-five individuals comprising all three groups had been evaluated by an impartial tester. Progress or regression in each case was studied and the psychometrist arbitrarily assigned a percentage of improvement to each person.

Definite relief of symptoms was, of course, visible to the eye. They were gratifying and, in some instances, dramatic. Migraine headaches, stuttering, ulcers had responded satisfactorily to psychotherapy but in the case of Prayer Therapy had been climaxed by total healing. The young professor who had retired because of tuberculosis and had then entered the Prayer Therapy Group was free of symptoms and planned to return to teaching in the Fall.

Thrilling as this evidence was, it was not sufficient for our academic purposes, thus the important thing was the result of the tests, the progress shown by groups as well as individuals after nine months of specific therapy.

The Overall Picture

Group I, those receiving individual psychotherapy with no mention of prayer or religion, made 65 per cent noticeable improvement in both tests and symptoms.

These results, from a psychologist's point of view, were excellent.

Group II, the Random Prayers, those who had prayed on their own every night without benefit of psychological insight, showed almost no progress in the tests, backsliding in some instances. Symptoms were not noticeably improved.

Group III, the Prayer Therapy group, however, made 72 per cent improvement with the degree of improvement greater in both symptoms and tests, including the dramatic healings previously mentioned which were quite obvious to their physicians as well as to those who had known them throughout the course.

Group   I—65% improvement (Psychotherapy)
Group II—No improvement (Random Prayers)
Group III—72% improvement (Prayer Therapy)

Comparing these results, even cautious examiners admitted it seemed conclusive that Prayer Therapy was not only a most effective healing agent but that prayer properly understood might be the single most important tool in the reconstruction of man's personality. There was strong indication that something was wrong with prayer as understood and practiced by the Random Prayers, who having "asked and received not," must somehow have unknowingly "asked amiss," where the Prayer Therapy students had "asked and received." Further, results indicated that Prayer Therapy provided something additional to psychology, supplied something that was missing to complete the healing process.

An interesting sidelight was that, while those helped by psychotherapy were now prepared to go their own way, the Prayer Therapy students, to a man, wished to come back the following year and help others as they themselves had been helped. It would appear that this latter technique had succeeded in turning the eye and ear of the student outward, toward his fellow man, for it is a sure thing that the eye turned inward does not heed or see the need for help.

Individual Cases

If the weight of evidence of the entire results confirmed the value of Prayer Therapy, it was the study of individual cases that proved most enlightening on the "hows" and "whys."

Of the three ineffectual men, two were helped: Bart and Rev. G. Jerry, the minister's son in the Random Prayer group, continued to have stiff unaccountable headaches, to quarrel with his parents and the world. His improvement in every field was negligible and, without his conscious knowledge, he still lived by the Will to Fail. He put a good deal of effort into it, and his constant effort manifested constant failure.

Bart, the bank employee, succeeded through personal counseling in recognizing this Will to Fail. He made a definite effort to adopt a more positive attitude, to face circumstances as they were and resolve them. He became acquainted with himself and his need to stop rationalizing and to approach everything with the idea that he need not fail. This led to a more masculine and assertive attitude at home, and a more cooperative frame of mind at his bank, and both situations improved. Although his progress was gratifying, Bart could not yet be called an integrated person. Self-confidence deserted him too rapidly and his practice in trusting himself broke down every time he discovered that he was all too fallible. Bart, unaided, could and *did* fail, and, with no Greater Power to turn to, each time he did fail, he was back in the old sewer, despondently trying to work his way out.

The Rev. G. in Prayer Therapy had ceased clicking his teeth and lost his nervous tic after three months, much to his and everyone else's relief. But his road had not been an easy one. When the first slips were passed out to the Prayer Therapy group, reactions varied from indignation, amazement, disbelief, to humble acceptance, as in Klaus' case. The gray-haired, imposing-looking minister found it hard to face the fact that he was "exacting, condescending, critical," and later that he was "not aware of people and their needs," that pride encompassed not only his "intellectual but spiritual life and built a wall around his willingness to receive . . ." But the crowning blow was to face a slip which stated bluntly that he needed "to be convinced of salvation through Christ" if he was to continue to preach it, or ever preach it successfully.

This was the big shake-up, the earthquake, for it forced him to quit kidding himself, drove him out of his fantasy world to view where he really stood and become willing to do something about it. The outside world he could not change. Himself, through prayer, he could. But he had to understand that we just can't get ourselves off our hands. Samuel Hoffenstein, in a nine-word "Proem," summed this up: "Wherever I go, *I* go too, and spoil everything."*

His first attempt to be honest uncovered the fact that he *feared* God. Taking the Biblical invitation, "Acquaint now thyself with me and be at peace," for his homework, he honestly sought to know more about God, to sense through prayer what He really was. Slowly he began to relate himself to others, to the universe and to a God of Love. Improvement then was rapid and, in the end, through honesty, prayer and meditation, he *found* God, as a living, loving Reality. Then there was nothing miraculous when he abandoned his personal attempt to run the whole show, when he permitted God to express Himself intelligently through others, or even when, at the age of sixty-one, he finally became pastor of another church in another parish, that long-desired "church of his own."

One of the saddest failures was that of Esther W., the teacher verging on a nervous breakdown, who had confidently entered the Random Prayer group. She had been so eager to participate and so sure she would prove what the power of her prayers could accomplish. Yet her retests showed no improvement, despite a good prognosis at the beginning. Although the sister-in-law whom she had blamed for much that was amiss in her daily life had long since left, she continued to feel that if others would only behave, she would have a better chance. She still felt the world was evil and the best chance for improve-

* *Pencil in the Air,* by Samuel Hoffenstein, Doubleday, 1947.

ment lay hereafter and proved this to herself by accepting depression and despondency in this world and escaping in daydreams to a fantasy world of the future
where there were no problems to face.

New physical symptoms in the form of asthma had
developed and, when I last heard of Esther, she had
been forced to abandon teaching and was being slowly
driven further from active life. She continued rigidly
in her pattern of conformity, refusing Prayer Therapy
as a new departure and showed no willingness or desire
to try anything that was not prescribed by and for everyone else.

It was quite the opposite, however, with Mabel McN.
who had been under personal counseling for much the
same reasons as Esther. At the end of the experiment,
Mabel had made some progress but it had been slow going and she had not yet reached the stage where therapy
could be discontinued.

She was no longer afraid of her own thoughts, had
faced the buried hostility and resultant guilt that had attacked her after her mother-in-law's death. She had made
strides in self-honesty, could admit that her world was
not "always lovely," and attempt to abandon blaming
others for all contrary conditions. But she still had strong
anxieties and fits of depression when she thought she
would be better off dead.

"I've gotten gobs of things out into my consciousness,"
she said. "But they don't just fade away and I don't know
what to do about them." Then, when she was still receiving individual counseling, some months after the
prayer experiment was concluded, she said sadly, "I've
been searching for something for years. If I could contact God and never let Him go, that is where I would
find happiness."

Mabel entered the next Prayer Therapy class. Prayer
Therapy supplied the integrating factor in her life, taught
her what to do with those detrimental things she had
gotten out into consciousness. As her confidence in God
increased, she lost her rigidity and was able to "loose
them and let them go."

Mrs. V. had found her freedom in the original Prayer Therapy class. It took some time, for she was determined, as Esther and Mabel had been, to find the fault and causes in other people, in circumstances, in anything that helped her believe her own inner household was still in perfect order. She resisted the fact that "rigidity, insistence on overconforming, keeping exactly with the Joneses" had robbed her of flexibility, individuality, self-expression and confidence. Could such seemingly small things, she demanded in a class discussion, cause such major troubles? The answer lay all about her. The grass and bushes and saplings will weather a tornado. The brittle dry tree will snap like a matchstick in a small wind. When the stresses and strains blew through life, the normal person swayed gently with the breeze. Mrs. V. snapped. She broke down, not once but three times. Responding only to social pressures and inflexible impersonal standards in the outer world, her inner world was static, brittle, and her inner resources entirely undeveloped. There was no life flow to keep her being supple, confident; there was no "give" to her and when attacked, when circumstances refused to conform, she did the only thing she could do—she went to pieces.

All this she rejected until a chance remark of a fellow student hit home. Mrs. V. had been describing to a foreman from a nearby iron foundry the weary preparations she was making for a visit from her son and daughter-in-law. His eyes twinkled as she detailed the backbreaking efforts she was expending. At last he said, "Are you always that much trouble to yourself?"

It was a piercing thrust. Later Mrs. V. told the class with amazing honesty that she had gone home and asked, in her prayers, "God, *am* I always that much trouble to myself? Am I always that much trouble to *You?*" The answer came, she reported, while she was looking through an inspirational book and found the words used by John Joseph Surin when asked why, when so many people undertake direct service to God, there are so few saints. "The chief reason," Surin replied, "is that they give too big a place in life to indifferent things."

Mrs. V. began to see that conforming was, in God's scheme, a very indifferent thing. When no two roses, people, not even two hairs on her head were alike, why try to conform? Was not originality, individuality, personality itself, God-given? Did her happiness lie in pleasing God or man? If she would cooperate with God, He would cooperate with her and in fulfilling His pattern there was no tension, no stress or strain. From that moment any thought of nervous breakdown was swept away and, as her prognosis had indicated, the minute her prayer life gave her the confidence to abandon "an imitation of life" for *living* it, she traveled the long road back to usefulness and abundant life.

As far as Mrs. V. had needed to travel, our friend Klaus had even further to come along the way opened up by Prayer Therapy. But his rate of progress was amazing and seemed to stem from his acute discomfort, his willingness from the beginning to go to any lengths to free himself, his conviction that the baggage he had been carrying had brought him nothing but pain and sorrow. With each successive slip he promptly and honestly searched out its truth within himself. And just as promptly set about trying to be rid of it. He was able to accept a concept of a God "who did not stand outside of living things" but was the Divine, Omnipresent Intelligence whose forward thrust was evolution itself. He appreciated immediately the idea that such an Intelligence would not launch creatures and creation and then send them off alone like an engineer who might set his train in motion and then let it career madly through the night without guidance. The engineer stayed in the cab and so God would stay with Klaus to guide and direct his progress.

Prayer then became his means of taking that guidance and direction. As a part of so great a scheme, as a participator, so to speak, in evolution itself, Klaus, over a period of months, was freed from his hostility, his fear, his feeling of inadequacy, and his honest attempts to cooperate with this Force released him from his burden of guilt.

During the course of the classes Klaus' epileptic seizures decreased steadily. When, one day, he was over-taken during a Prayer Therapy session, the class stood by and prayed simply and quietly and when he recovered he found no horror, no condemnation, nothing but understanding and the desire to help among those who had witnessed his attack. The class itself gained an awareness of the *power* of loving one's neighbor as oneself because it was from that moment of complete acceptance by his fellow man that Klaus began to lose his fear of the seizures and a large measure of his resentment and hostility. Months went by before a recurrence. By the end of our nine months of study, he was freed of the sedation habit and in the last eighteen years has not had a single epileptic seizure.

With his acceptance of all gifts as God-given and innocent under His guidance, his family atmosphere relaxed. He was able to adopt a normal attitude toward sex relations. His wife had followed his Prayer Therapy work with the intensity and longing which loneliness and fear breed in the hearts of women who love and live with those men who are destroying themselves and seem hell bent toward extinction. She was able to help him.

Klaus' retests showed a man reborn, traveling daily toward more abundant life. This time he told the tester he had found his direction in the inspirational words of the *Theologia Germanica*, "I would fain be to the Eternal Goodness, what his own hand is to man." With this goal before him, Klaus' life today has that purpose which he asked at the beginning, and he feels a greater degree of fulfillment of both the inner and outer man.

Where Prayer and Psychology Failed

After the final personal interviews, using reason and logic along with the evidence, there was strong evidence as to the missing pieces of psychology and what was wrong with random prayer.

In the case of Mabel McN. who, while helped by psychotherapy, was healed only when she turned to Prayer Therapy, it was obvious that *man unaided failed.* "All you need is self-confidence" proved no more effective with her, even when shown the reasons underlying her lacks, than it had with Bart. What was self-confidence to be based upon? Only as she found herself related to God, herself as the image, the child or offspring of the Divine, did she have anything solid in which to base the needed confidence.

Klaus had failed to overcome hostility and resentments and fears for the simple reason that, alone, he remained unrelated, an alien in the universe and among men. The well-integrated man is secure in his relationships with himself, his fellows and the world. Klaus had found nothing to supply this relationship, no central Unity.

Once God and evolution were reconciled in his mind, he could take those flaws to which psychiatry had alerted him over many weary years without effecting a healing, and talk with God through prayer, confident that God, directing His great evolution, would not allow His work to be sabotaged where there was willingness to cooperate. God *gave* him the necessary help to become His instrument and his relationship to a Supreme Being, an All-Powerful Force for Good, related Klaus to all things, including his neighbor.

An ever present danger in personal therapy was the tendency of the patient to become overly dependent on the therapist. The Prayer Therapy Group, while using the psychological tests for insight, came to recognize the Divine within themselves as an ever present source of help which had a constant advantage over a human being, no matter how wise, loving or clever a therapist might be.

Psychology and the modern mind sciences then had proved themselves an invaluable tool for insight but alone didn't complete the treatment any more than the X-ray which located the broken bone can be held responsible for setting it.

In the case of the Random Pray*ers*, however, the need for this insight was all too evident. In no case had the individual succeeded in searching out the maladjustments which tests indicated to be responsible for his emotional upsets.

In their confession or examination of conscience not one seemed to go beyond the obvious broken moral laws and blanketing their feelings of guilt by constant affirmation that they were "miserable sinners," totally unworthy, offering their subconscious a steady diet of self-condemnation, self-pity, and hopelessness. Hopeless they were too, for apparently the God of whom they asked forgiveness never granted it. Over and over, as a child might beg for water from a stone, they craved forgiveness and one can only assume the response was negative and the effort useless and beamed toward an unwilling or unlistening ear.

Their form of prayer was negative as well, in complete violation of the definite instruction to pray "believing ye have received and ye shall receive." But that promise was fulfilled because as they reiterated their unhappy symptoms, holding them directly in the focus of their minds, reaffirming them, they held them firmly in place and did not let them go. What they believed, they got. Negative prayer produced negative results.

Jerry, the minister's son, used rote prayer for the most part, reiterated his guilt and his "wormy feelings," constantly asked forgiveness which he never took. His concept of God was a faraway Being which increased his sense of dependence and inadequacy because he could never be sure He was listening. Each night he confirmed his symptoms, his discontent, his hopelessness, following this with a positive statement that he wasn't worthy of anything better, and for 271 evenings straight told God and himself what a failure they made as a team.

The young schoolteacher, Esther, who had had such high hopes in her prayer power, only to be completely disappointed, had a concept of God which we found among many of the Random Prayers. God, to her, was a *just* God, a God of wrath and, like Rev. G., she feared Him. It was interesting to note that she drew this concept from the use of the word Father more than from the Old Testament of the Bible. It speaks well for St.

Joseph that Jesus of Nazareth was able to employ this human term Father for the transcendent relationship between man and his Maker. But Esther's father, as we recall, had been a just man, rigid and very religious. He also had been critical, unloving, without understanding, warmth or praise. Esther, then, was stuck with a Father God who was not much of an improvement over her earthly father. To some degree it was a comparable, if reversed story of the little girl who asked a friend if she believed there was a devil. "Of course not," her friend replied. "It's just like Santa Claus. It's only your father."

Nor had she been able through self-examination to bring into consciousness the feelings of insecurity, her fantasy world, her determination to blame others, the fear of sex and rigid desire to conform which, her tests indicated, were causing her neurotic condition, rendering her useless to the God whom she would serve. She did, however, believe that she, like the rest of the world, was "wicked," which was far from the truth, but this blanket admission spared her the necessity of taking an honest and probably painful inventory of her actual emotional content.

She accepted her sufferings as a punishment or lesson and, in her actual prayer feelings, resigned herself to it with such a complete acceptance that it was not surprising she could not hope for a better deal from her God through any other type of prayer. In spite of the fact that her prognosis had been good, that repression or the loss of talents could well be a sin against the Holy Ghost, she preferred to "fear" Him now, accept her suffering, and maybe in the great by-and-by when things got better, she would love Him and He would treat her kindly.

Other interviews with the Random Prayers simply confirmed these attitudes and views. They began with an act of self-condemnation (a far cry from true confession with accompanying forgiveness), followed this with negative prayer, their concept of God wavering between a God of wrath visiting them with punishment and martyrdom and a far-off Being busy with Cosmic

Affairs who might possibly hear them if they cried loudly enough.

These techniques and concepts were diametrically opposed to those developed and used with such marked success by the Prayer Therapy group. Here was the answer for the banker who came to my office saying, "I'm from Arizona . . . but you've still got to show me!"

After five years more of experiments, dropping the control groups which had served their purpose, we were ready to answer the queries of thousands more who wanted the actual unfoldments and procedures which had proved scientifically in an academic laboratory that prayer, properly understood and practiced, could change the individual life anywhere, any time, at any age. It blended with any organized religion and still was open to the agnostic. It fitted any pocketbook. Since the original experiment, three hundred persons had found, through the methods detailed in subsequent chapters, the answer to *how* we could change direction, walk away from extinction, and toward serenity, physical and mental well-being, to more victorious living.

4

THE KINGDOM WITHIN

DR. CARL JUNG, THE GREAT SWISS PIONEER OF THE Age of Psychology, states that man "has only to realize that he is shut up inside his mind and cannot step beyond it, even in insanity; and that the appearance of his world or his gods very much depends upon his own mental condition." That is modern phraseology.

Christ Jesus said it more simply. "The kingdom of God, of heaven, is within you."

Conversely, what about the kingdom of hell?

William James, renowned American psychologist and philosopher, answers: "The hell to be endured hereafter, of which theology tells, is no worse than the hell we make ourselves in this world by habitually fashioning our characters in the wrong way."

If both kingdoms are within us, in our mind or consciousness, then may we not choose to unlock either the one or the other—to dwell in heaven, harmony, well-being, or in chaos, confusion, suffering?

Immediately the answer comes: "I certainly do not choose to be depressed, fearful, nervous, to have migraine or ulcers!" Klaus, in our Prayer Therapy experiment, had not consciously chosen epilepsy, drugs, alcoholism as his portion in life. However, the first step seemed to be to accept the fact that the causes, whether active with or without our full consent, were definitely within. Jesus said so. Modern psychology says so. And, furthermore, our experiments had proven it to us. Then, if the cause was within, the cure had to be within. We proved that as well.

Both John the Baptist and Jesus insisted that we "repent," for "the kingdom of heaven is at hand." And the literal translation of that word is to "have another mind." To do this we found we had to make a searching and fearless journey into the kingdom within, to have a look at the present furnishings, be able to recognize what we must be rid of before we could hope to establish internal harmony.

It is true that no man knowingly chooses to become useless, ill, a burden to himself. But ignorance of the laws governing the internal world, good intentions with which hell is proverbially paved, even clean living and "being good," had not been sufficient to help Jerry, the minister's son, nor Esther, the young schoolteacher, nor thirteen other Random Prayers to escape just such manifestations. To most of us this inner region is as dark and unexplored as Dr. Livingstone's Africa into which the most well-meaning prayer cannot penetrate without a map, a guide.

In 400 B.C. Socrates issued his famous challenge, "Know Thyself." Jesus was even more explicit, "Ye shall know the truth and the truth shall make you free." The Nazarene drew an instant protest from his listeners. "We are free," they said. "We were freeborn and we are not slaves." Humanly, in the external world, this was true. So he must have had reference to *his* kingdom, the one "not of this world," but "within you." He did not speak of freedom from chains and whips and servitude in the material world but of freedom from the chains and whips of fear, tension, worry, depression that keep us in mental and emotional bondage and drag us toward a veritable hell on earth.

Why do we submit? Because, so far, few of us have learned *how* to know the truth about ourselves even should we wish it. And most of us are actually afraid to look. There may be buried treasure within, but we also suspect that there may be a good deal of rubbish. It is distasteful, even painful, to dig it out and look at it, and the individual reaction to such exploration is to see only the pretty scenery and ignore the dark corners.

There is no deception quite so great as self-deception, nor quite so dangerous!

It is well to remember, before we shrink away from the need to "find out what we have to work with even if it hurts" as our friend, Klaus, put it, that man has no faculties for forgetting, only remembering. Still, we can and do hide from ourselves. Again, *why?*

Primarily because we are afraid of being condemned, either by ourselves or others. On the one hand, our self-esteem would be blasted. On the other, people wouldn't like us. They would judge or condemn. We know that for a fact. Don't we ourselves judge and condemn others? And so, while we cannot forget, we can bury what is displeasing and leave it to fester in bodily or neurotic symptoms. But make no mistake about it. Until we uproot it, it is still there. So the first actual step we took in Prayer Therapy was to *make prayer a practice in honesty.*

The Key to the Kingdom

The guides we used, once we had accepted this Key as the gateway to the kingdom within, will be detailed in later chapters. But we found we first had to believe that this *was* the Key and we *must* use it, must honestly look within. Until we do, we have little insight into what drives us, or why; in other words, no conscious control over our decisions and actions. Our outward selves will be automatons following deeply hidden unconscious patterns and we will in no wise be that entity with free will and self-choice in which we all believe.

Is that hard to accept? Do we think we are in the driver's seat during all our waking moments? Take the successful young orange rancher, a man with a comfortable income, easy rural life, charming wife and children, who entered our Prayer Therapy experiment when a well-known medical clinic recommended an operation to remove a portion of his stomach. There was no worry-tension pattern here to account for his painful ulcer.

Certainly he could, and did, deny that he had chosen an ulcer. Consciously, of course, he had not. But with the prod of slips which I formulated from his first psychological tests, he began to see what he had chosen. One said, "He is almost bitterly critical of human beings. Feels everyone has let him down." Another, "He dare not really evaluate himself. He is afraid to face the resentment and hostility he has built up over imagined and real slights."

Bitter criticism! Hostility! Fear! Since guilt buried these deep within, they did not manifest as enmity toward his fellow man but as ulcer symptoms. Later he told the class, "No one likes to think they are capable of hating, certainly not on a large scale. If my ulcer hadn't been tremendously uncomfortable, I'd probably have gone home permanently after my first slip."

Here was the value in that warning pain. He had to face it, to recognize that hate, hostility, bitterness, criticism had been his driving forces for years, whether he had known it or not.

"My first step was to take the dare," he said. "To realize that a negative emotion does not grow from being looked at . . . and to be honest with myself." In other words, to *make prayer a practice in honesty*.

If you think that isn't a tall order, wait until you have finished the chapter on the Four Demons and Chapters 11 and 12, and then try it. Approached fearlessly it can cause a veritable earthquake in that inner kingdom. Remember, we are not going to stop there. The young orange grower admitted that simply seeing the dark spots, the hidden drives behind his mask, didn't rid him of his problems or effect a complete change of attitudes. That came later through direct use of prayer. But it did give him the opportunity to make a conscious choice, alerted him to what he had chosen in the past. He did not, at that point, become what he wished to be, what God intended he should be. He simply discovered what he was and what he did *not* wish to be.

The first step requires only a willingness to see what we honestly entertain in our mental household. The normal reaction on glimpsing a dark corner is to return promptly to the noisy everyday world and turn on the television, to "let sleeping dogs lie." We think it is easier to stay with the crowd, to place our attention only on the things which touch the five senses, forgetting Jung's point that the appearance of this world, our reaction to it, plus our own growth toward maturity, our bodily health, our very spiritual evolution, depends, not on this outer, but on the inner world. "The kingdom of heaven is within you!"

If we would alter our lives, the first change must come within ourselves, within the realm of consciousness. Now, what do we know about the Human Consciousness?

Hypnotism and the Unconscious

Below the level of our thinking reasoning mind, the conscious mind that has been conditioned by education, environment, experience, lies a great stream of consciousness of which we are, for the most part, unaware.

As it has varying depths, facets and interpreters, so it has many names. Just below the surface is a stratum which Jung has called the personal unconscious where the individual stores rejected memories and emotional material. This murky region which we furnish ourselves stands between us and the deeper levels of the subconscious acting as a sort of dictator in both directions. The actual great stream of consciousness beyond it contains, not only our heritage of instincts and patterns from the entire race, but the ability to act on suggestions made to it. For most of us this is a rather involved theory and the evidence is hearsay. Have we any concrete examples which testify to the existence and power of this invisible but talented unconscious and to how it takes dictation?

One way to view both is when the conscious, conditioned mind, with all its veto power, superstitions, fears, etc., is in abeyance. This condition is fulfilled in hypnotism.

F. W. H. Myers in his *Human Personality** gives a typical instance where an inexperienced young understudy was suddenly called on to take over the star's role in a theatrical company. She was quite literally overcome with stage fright and felt she could not go on. Under light hypnosis, however, she went through the part brilliantly and received excellent critical notices.

The function of hypnosis here is, first, to set the conscious mind with its inhibitions at rest, to cut through the murky personal unconscious with its buried memories of past failures, and then call upon the great subconscious to deliver by the use of auto-suggestion. And it does deliver!

It is also possible to prove beyond the shadow of a doubt, the effect of suggestion upon the physical body by means of hypnosis. In an experiment in which I participated, the subject under hypnosis, a young man of twenty-five, was asked if he would like to smoke. The hypnotist, instead of giving him a cigarette, handed him a long piece of chalk which the subject accepted and began to draw upon exactly as though he were smoking. Asked if he liked the brand, he replied that he did. After a bit, the hypnotist said in a tense, frightened tone, "Look out. It's burning your finger." Immediately the young man dropped the chalk and complained that his finger hurt. The hypnotist suggested that he had burned it. When we examined the finger, a blister had appeared where he had been holding the chalk, and where no blister had been before.

Obviously the young man's mind was free from the conscious, habitual belief that chalk does not burn and cigarettes do, for not only did he mentally accept the suggestion, but *his body accepted it* and obediently manifested burns.

There are countless examples of physical strength in weak individuals, of remarkable courage in those with particular fears, as the man who fears high places but will walk a narrow elevated plank under hypnosis, again at-

---

* *Human Personality and Its Survival of Bodily Death,* by F. W. H. Myers, Longmans, Green & Co., Inc.

testing to the fact that, when negative blocks are removed, the subconscious functions harmoniously and independently to produce the desired results.

Yet hypnotism is no cure-all for the ills of the world. It is by no means a new art nor is its usage unknown to psychology and psychiatry. Let us examine the uses Freud made of it and why he abandoned it in favor of conscious analysis and suggestion.

Half a century ago Sigmund Freud, the first pioneer of medical psychology as we know it today, took up the challenge of converting this science from a mechanical study of the lobes and divisions of the brain and intricacies of the physical nervous system, to a study of mind or consciousness.

In the beginning Freud was using hypnosis to keep the inhibited cautious conscious mind quiet while he probed for causes and directed suggestions to the unconscious.

Ernest R. Trattner in his outline on Freud* reports that Freud, after a short time, began to find drawbacks in the hypnotic technique. "It often afforded only temporary relief," he writes. "It was, besides, dangerous, for persons hypnotized too often had a tendency to acquire a mental lassitude and general predisposition that made them susceptible to the slightest suggestion on the part of the physician, even when they were in a normal waking state."

Freud had discovered that conscious techniques, while sometimes requiring more effort on the part of the therapist, got better and more lasting results when, according to Trattner, "an incident occurred which precipitated his decision. A female patient whom he had had under hypnotic treatment for some time suddenly threw her arms about his neck on awakening from a trance, and a most embarrassing situation might have arisen, if the unexpected entrance of a servant had not cleared the air. Freud wanted no more of such incidents, which

---

* *Architects of Ideas,* by Ernest R. Trattner, Carrick & Evans, Inc., 1938.

he had absolutely no way of foreseeing from the information gathered in the hypnotic treatment."

While hypnosis under trained experts still has definite therapeutic value in specific cases such as shell shock, it is no easy magic and should definitely be a preserve posted against the non-scientific amateur.

We will take time right here to say that analysis in the Freudian sense is not for the amateur either and, when misunderstood or mishandled, can undoubtedly do more harm than good. At no time in this book will we suggest or encourage depth analysis by the individual, for those who are seriously mentally or emotionally disturbed need expert help; what we aim to show is how the rest of us who are leading "lives of quiet desperation," displaying psychosomatic symptoms, or generally feel that our daily existence is not all it should be, can acquire the ability to make prayer a practice in honesty, to know the truth about ourselves as the first step toward freedom.

In reviewing the evidence for the power of the unconscious as it relates to hypnotism, there is still one facet we should regard. The suggestion here ensues as the act of one mind affecting another. Let us assume that this is a "good" well-meaning mind, even possibly an intelligent and wise one, and we do know for a fact that no hypnotized person can be induced to *do* anything violently opposed to his own will and natural character. Yet a change of any sort wrought by hypnotism, however beneficial, *has not changed your conscious mind,* nor yet even brought you closer to our first step, self-honesty. The young actress who was able to perform under light hypnotism which suggested to her the removal of her fears had not actually lost them. She continued to depend on hypnotism and the hypnotist was present in her dressing room to direct her thinking throughout many weeks. She was only freed of this dependence when post-hypnotic suggestion was substituted.

None of this helps us toward our goal of taking full possession of ourselves, finding out what we have to work with, and then proceeding to work out our own salvation.

Nor is hypnotism the only method of viewing the power of the subconscious. We get an equally if not more dramatic result sometimes when the mind and emotions are fully under some unusual demand or pressure which jolts us out of our habitual thought patterns or educated beliefs in our limitations.

Glimpses of Our Hidden Power

On the negative side we have examples provided by Dr. Alexis Carrel.* "Emotions," he says, "induce, in especially sensitive individuals, striking modifications of the tissues and humors. The hair of a Belgian woman condemned to death by the Germans became white during the night preceding the execution. On the arm of another woman, an eruption appeared during a bombardment. After the explosion of each shell, the eruption became redder and larger."

On the positive side there are innumerable examples of men and women, fully conscious but under great pressure, rising to accomplishments of which their everyday selves appear incapable. Almost any man who experienced the last World War saw dramatic first-hand instances of this. Recently our newspapers reported a case where a woman had been hit by a car and pinned under the front end. The spectators who gathered were making hasty plans to lift the automobile when a Negro stepped from the crowd and, before over a hundred witnesses, alone and unaided, lifted the car so that the woman could be pulled to safety. On the following day reporters asked him to lift the same car so that the photographers could make pictures. He was unable to budge it. A crisis would seem to raise us temporarily above thoughts of limitation and fear and tap hidden resources *already there and waiting to be utilized*.

Another interesting bit of evidence is offered by Dr.

---

* *Man, the Unknown,* by Alexis Carrel, Harper & Brothers, 1935.

E. R. Carlson.* Dr. Carlson, a seriously involved spastic, not only became an M.D. but a surgeon. It wasn't until he was ready for college that he persuaded authorities in grade school to erase from his record the term "mentally retarded." Not only was he spastic, but he had the tenseness and tremor that often appear in such cases. However, when he was ready to make a surgical incision, he was completely steady, all tremor and tenseness left him and he was able to perform with great skill.

What the deep mind desires apparently the body will cooperate to do. That is what makes our study of our real attitudes and desires, our hidden emotions and thoughts, of immediate and vital importance to us. We are now, this minute, getting direct results from them.

If we don't like the results we will have to effect a change within. Now, we have admitted that we do not consciously "desire" many of the things we suffer. But what is our conscious mind putting into the burial ground of the personal unconscious, there to ferment and dictate the "appearance of our world and our gods"? To make prayer a practice in honesty we must know how to look within and what we are looking for.

---

* *Born That Way,* by E. R. Carlson, The John Day Company, Inc., 1941.

5

THE FOUR DEMONS

PSYCHOLOGY RECOGNIZES FOUR PRINCIPLE TROUBLE-
makers in the realm of the personal unconscious. They
are Fear, Guilt, Inferiority Feelings, Misguided Love
(Hate). In our Prayer Therapy class as members gained
confidence and began to share the content of their secret
slips, the individual took much consolation in finding
that scarcely any of them were immune and most had a
touch of all four demons, making a vicious circle in
consciousness.

Earlier we mentioned the young orange grower whose
ulcer symptoms had been traced to roots of hostility, bitterness and fear. Exactly how did the four demons operate in his case? Once he had accepted the dare, begun
to make prayer a practice in honesty, his inventory admitted the presence of these negative governing forces.
Next, he was forced to ask *why?*

The Vicious Circle

He saw a pattern of himself as a youngster, working
parents, busy older brothers; a strong feeling that he was
neglected, unwanted (Inferiority). Though they showed
no interest in him he deeply wanted to love them, to
have them love him, and this lack and a growing bitterness caused shame which he tried to conceal from others
and succeeded finally in concealing from himself

(Guilt). Nebulous fears grew and he protected himself with hostility, bitterness (Hate).

At the close of the class he made a statement we were all to remember. "Today," he said, "remembering how violently I guarded my own soft spot, I'm pretty tolerant. I know hostility comes from underneath where pain and fear are, not from meanness. When you find a touch of one demon you usually recognize a touch of them all. The strongest one, in my case Hate, disguised as bitterness and hostility, was merely where I entered the circle for purposes of eviction."

This eviction process will be detailed in a later chapter but now let us examine the demons one by one, so that we will be able to recognize them in ourselves.

Fear: the Skeleton in the Closet

One of the first problems to be faced by each of us is fear. It is a well-known medical fact that fear reacts on the endocrine glands causing dysfunction of the whole system. Generally speaking, we are born with two fears: fear of falling and fear of loud noises. By the time we reach maturity we may have accumulated dozens of fears: fear of the dark, fear of high places, fear of closed places, fear of going to sleep, fear of snakes, spiders, water, fear of death and so on.

But, at the head of the list, in the order of their detrimental effect on us, we must place fear of our own thoughts. We cannot afford to think of ourselves or see ourselves as we actually are. We deny certain thoughts and feelings. Inner honesty, as we have said before, is too painful. This denial is "ego protection" and this "ego protection" can keep a person a prisoner within the realms of their own mind. This means that doors within the mind must be kept closed. The skeleton in the closet must not be seen by the conscious mind or others and here we create the block between the conscious and the talented unconscious and set up a turbulent no-man's land between the two. The doors leading from this buffer state are free to swing outward to the conscious or inward to the subconscious. Energy from the conscious is used to lean against them to keep unwanted material buried while pressure from the subconscious tries to release its burden. Thus the first job in overcoming the fear of one's thoughts is to recognize that pushing them down, submerging them, doesn't do a thing for us.

Why is the ego so defensive? Why do we have a tendency to put ourselves in the best possible light? The natural spontaneous desires of early childhood come in conflict with the environment. A child starts building an ego and, about the same time, a super-ego (conscience). The ego becomes the defense against the environment. Right here we begin the practice of self-deceit. From early childhood we are told to be careful what we say. We learn that, if we say some things, we get into trouble. Shortly we learn that it is better not even to think them. It becomes almost impossible for us to go through a day being absolutely honest. We unconsciously shove undesirables out of sight . . . but they are there.

One of the loveliest ladies to enter the original Prayer Therapy experiment was Claudia R. Brilliant intellectually, she had drifted through college on an academic scholarship. Later she had been a successful actress, drama instructor at two large colleges, was well married with a handsome young daughter. Outwardly she seemed a charming, successful, self-possessed woman in every way. She could control her emotions behind a tight, bright smile but her body was betraying her with bouts of sciatica, migraine headaches, low blood pressure, dizziness and a positively mid-Victorian talent for fainting. Through her slips, "emotional immaturity, tensions, fears, more guilt than anyone I have ever examined," she at length came to the place where she could admit that she "had suffered the tortures of the damned for years through inferiority, guilt, and a fear of people and their opinions. It is no good," she added, "being outwardly successful if you are inwardly miserable."

But the tremendous block that had to be melted away was her very real fear of her own thoughts. As a child she had had a well-meaning aunt who used to look at her two older sisters, real beauties, and then shake her head at Claudia and say, "Well, you'll never be a beauty so you'll have to be *good.*" Her mother affirmed this and, stressing her intellectual brightness, added, "You must *succeed.*" Between trying so hard to be *good* and to *succeed,* which to her meant one and the same thing, she became simply unnatural, dishonest with herself and particularly, since she was a very devout girl, dishonest with God. Above all things, before she tried to stand in His presence, she must wear her "good girl" face and only tell Him the *good* things she had thought or done. Her real release came when I happened to write on the bottom of one of her confidential slips, "Don't be afraid to talk it over with God. He knows it anyway . . . and understands."

With many of us the basis for ninety per cent of our fears is our own wishes, projections, coming back at us. Ill will, resentment, hostility, envy quickly buried by that alert sentinel, the conscious mind, come back to us as fear. Jesus knew exactly what He was suggesting when He insisted that we forgive our enemies, promptly, unto 70 times 7, *before* carrying our prayers to the altar. This law, if practiced by all who profess to Christianity, would psychologically prevent much of our fear.

As it is, the fears that come back to us will seem greater, more horrible, more intolerable than they actually were because the super-ego magnifies. Whatever fear it is then that possesses us, it must be realized that it is magnified, and it will seem worse than was actually the case in the beginning.

Any psychologist will discount fifty per cent of that "terrible whipping" a patient received as a child. His size at the time, plus the magnification of the super-ego in 99 cases out of a hundred, have done quite a job on what was probably just a fair-to-middling spanking.

I recently had a medical doctor who admitted that, although he had smoked for years, he had never smoked in front of his mother because he was still terrified by the memory of her strict punishment. She was a frail little lady, had never been robust, and my personal knowledge of her precluded such violence as he recalled.

With the help of his conscience he had magnified these things until he was much harder on himself than she had ever been.

If we do not bury our ill will, if we do not rid ourselves of it by forgiveness, but give it expression in our lives, then again we are afraid for, as hate or resentment or envy go out from us as thought or expression, so they come back to us from others and we fear the consequences of our own acts.

Fears are pre-symptomatic warnings. If the fear is pushed out of the conscious mind, suppressed, one's friends and family are apt to say we are more grown up, more mature, less scatterbrained. And, if a method for ridding oneself of them had been developed, this would be true. But if they are merely buried we can develop symptoms to cope with the feelings such as stuttering, abdominal pains, high blood pressure, a tic, an allergy, or a taste for drink. The symptoms, however, are not as dangerous or as damaging to the personality as complete suppression of the fear with no release. Here we have a volcanic block in that no-man's land which may erupt suddenly or simply drive us farther and farther away from real life.

Fear is the motivating power behind all repressions and suppressions. Guilty fears, the fear of being found out or exposed, of being humiliated, commonly called an "anxiety neurosis," are tremendously damaging and the need here, as with all fear, is to bring the object of dread into the full light and face it. If confession or private examination of conscience can be candid enough, then suppression and repression are overcome.

But the person who clings to these buried fears will often become inactive. The imagination of the inactive person is in free-wheeling and there is no limit to what he will conjure up with his mind.

John Dollard, outstanding psychologist at Yale University,* has listed seven kinds of foolish fears which are common to many of us:

Fear of:

1. Failure
2. Sex
3. Self-defense
4. Trusting others
5. Thinking
6. Speaking
7. Being alone

Let's take each one into the light and examine it.

Fear of Failure: inwardly thinking that one is inferior, small or weak, causes some not to try at all, to give up easily. All of us have such feelings at some time and obviously, when we do, we are defeated before we begin.

Fear of Sex: causes many to suffer real pain. So much of our training has been to fear or misunderstand anything and everything to do with sex feelings that this fear is easily mixed with guilt. A large number of married people are actually afraid of sex and do not take advantage of their freedom to cement their relationship within the framework of this natural and normal expression of married love. Although today's parents and clergy feel themselves enlightened on this subject, the enlightenment is often only intellectual and emotionally there is still a deep-seated mistrust and a clumsiness in dealing with it. Possibly because this drive misguided (as with all strong drives) turns violent or cheap, leads to dark alleys, it seems almost impossible for those responsible for a child's attitude toward sex to deal with it as the natural, beautiful thing the Creator must have meant it to be.

To begin to overcome the foolish fear of sex the individual must determine whether fear is causing his behavior and weed out all its disguises whether they appear as frigidity, morality, selfishness, or what not. The iden-

* *Victory Over Fear*, by John Dollard, Reynal and Hitchcock, Inc., 1942.

tification of the impulse that gives rise to the fear logically follows and, once identified, we are ready to take steps to respond wholesomely.

Fear of Self-Defense: stems from a loss of self-respect, and is failure to defend one's own rights and insist on a fair share of things. The tendency is to suffer in silence while resentment grows within. With many there is a confusion here with the religious principles involved. Meekness and humility, in the sense that Christ Jesus taught them, do not deny us the right to be Sons of God and joint heirs with Christ. In fact, He made it imperative that we make this identification.

Let us take the example of a woman, an asthmatic who came to one of our Prayer Therapy classes and was actually aware that her husband was involved in an extramarital affair with a woman she knew well. Tina was, however, suffering it in "Christian meekness and charity." To most of us this is a shocking misuse of the idea of charity, yet it is more possible than we think. In this particular case, the woman rated herself too low, her concept of herself being far short of a child of God, made in His image and likeness. There is no religious call for us to minimize our self-confidence or self-respect. In actuality, this woman had accepted, since childhood, all manner of deficiencies and shortcomings for herself. As a child, she had been severely punished for every type of naughtiness and, when any aggressive behavior on her part was met with violent counter-aggression, her very size made it impossible for her to defend herself.

Once she recognized her fear of self-defense as an insult to her God-given personality, she was ready to take the steps that led her back to the self-evaluation that was her birthright. Her husband yielded to her new concept of herself, and their marriage could proceed on a harmonious basis.

Fear of Trusting Others: is a repeated flaw in our dealings in human relations. "Don't depend on others and you won't be disappointed." Or "If you want something done, do it yourself." A young man who had found himself living in a friendless vacuum admitted that he "protected himself by anticipating that everyone would let him down (which they usually did), criticized them before they could catch him off guard and thus hurt or disappoint him." And then, because he had few friends, felt he was justified in his feelings. During his experience in World War II, he desperately wanted to become an officer, but soon found that the best officers were the men who could delegate authority with confidence, as well as lead. He found that his very life depended on trusting someone else . . . whether he wanted to or not . . . and so life itself thrust upon him the experience of trusting. He adjusted to it slowly, but once he did, he got his chance at OCS and became a fine officer.

Fear of Thinking and the *Fear of Speaking:* come to us all at some time, based mostly on that education of the conscious which causes so many of our inhibitions. We are punished for whispering in school and we have all gone through the agony of dreaming or imagining some undesirable thought or word escaping us in church or at a social gathering. One unguarded moment might reveal or betray what is behind the mask we present to the world.

The fear of thinking increases with a small degree of understanding that our thoughts affect our outer world. But further understanding releases us from this fear. We find it is the thoughts we harbor, hold onto, affirm, reiterate, in other words, those we give our attention to, or keep by burying, that have an effect. Everyone, even those whom we call saints where they admit constant vigilance, are attacked by so-called "wrong thoughts." The important thing to remember is that, recognized and properly disposed of, they have *absolutely no power to harm.* Unless we understand this, we shall become more and more afraid of our own thinking. Race consciousness and the powerful suggestions to which we are all open today will throw "foul balls" at us but it is up to us whether we catch them and put them into play, or whether we recognize them for what they are and refuse them. It is absolutely true that what *gets your attention, gets you.* But it has to *get your attention.*

Sometimes this is all too obvious in the little slips of the tongue that startle or amuse. One of my favorite examples is told on the charming Morrow family by Louis Untermeyer. Mrs. Dwight Morrow was entertaining at tea the great financier, J. P. Morgan. Her two daughters, one now Anne Morrow Lindbergh of literary fame, were to make an appearance and Mrs. Morrow, knowing young Anne's usual candor, developed a temporary fear of her daughter's speaking since Mr. Morgan had a nose which was large in size, brilliant in hue, a perfect target for childish forthrightness or curiosity. Before her guest's arrival, Mrs. Morrow indirectly briefed both girls on the social necessity of not calling attention to a guest's odd or unusual appearance.

Mr. Morgan duly arrived and the young ladies behaved with admirable restraint and were safely dispatched to their youthful activities. Whereupon Mrs. Morrow heaved a sigh of relief, turned to her tea urn, and asked graciously, "Mr. Morgan, will you have one or two lumps of sugar in your nose?"

What happened to Mrs. Morrow, the nightmare of the social slip, can and has happened to all of us. We see and laugh at its inception. Sometimes such fears are dreamed away where we appear at the Metropolitan Opera House in our night dress on a bicycle. But, carried a degree further, we have a buried fear which can produce stuttering and irrational behavior.

Those with a marked fear of thinking or speaking are overly dependent, submissive, often quite suggestible. When too many of them appear in a race, they can easily be deprived of the freedom of speech and will readily submit to a dictator who promises to do all their thinking for them, thus eliminating the fear.

Fear of Being Alone: is one of the most common. We can all recall being isolated, sent to our room as a punishment. Threats of abandonment are not uncommon. Where it is pronounced, this fear makes a restless, anxious individual constantly seeking company and distraction and little serenity is in sight. It can be limiting in the extreme, for most creative ideas, meditation, prayer, reverie, profound or even carefully directed thinking can only come to full flower when we are free to relax in our own company, away from "the world, its turmoil and its fitfulness," upon occasions.

The wise person will honestly examine himself and admit the fears he recognizes. Recognition and admission are the beginning of self-honesty and a subsequent solution. Remember that fear drains the body of needed energy, often causes us to expend more than we replenish, and the cells of the body actually suffer. Remember, too, that although our particular fears may seem absurd to many people, to us they can cause great mental and physical anguish. Once recognized we will be ready to take the definite steps for their elimination detailed in later chapters.

Guilt, Normal and Abnormal

Each of us possesses some guilt feelings and it should be emphasized from the beginning that our concern is not with *normal guilt*.

Right here we might take a look at the Laws by which the Universe and Man seem to operate. All thinking people are agreed that the Universe is run by "natural" laws. These are dependable, determinable, good. Man, too, when he is functioning adequately, is run by laws which we think of as Divine—not man-made. They are very different from, for instance, traffic laws, where, if you break one and no one is injured and you are not caught, there is no effect. These Divine laws are not as obvious, yet they *cannot* be broken without an effect upon ourselves and usually upon others as well. We do not break a Divine law but break ourselves *on* that law.

An elderly woman who entered our Prayer Therapy group had been consistently, if unconsciously, breaking the Law of Love. Mrs. S. herself was convinced that her extreme nervousness, weakness, tensions, arthritis, general ill-health were a necessary part of advancing years. She was studying Prayer Therapy, she said, on the advice of her clergyman to "enlarge her concept of prayer and

increase her power of *helping others change their lives*."
I had a personal acquaintance with her minister and was
aware that he had other hopes from her study. In his
opinion, her lack of ability to recognize her driving motives was not only ruining her own life, but those of her
son and daughter-in-law. Her reaction to her original slips
was one of extreme anger when they revealed that she
had been breaking the law of love in a good many directions. In order to build her own ego and sense of waning
usefulness, she found fault with everything her daughter-
in-law did. She belittled her constantly, tried to convince
her son that their financial position was due to the
younger woman's mismanagement, until her relationship
with them passed the point of the humorous mother-in-
law and became an actual menace. Mrs. S. was developing what her son called "a just-plain-mean streak."

One of her slips read, "She is *enjoying* disorders and
miseries, seeks pity as a means of attracting sympathy
and attention (substitutes for love)." Yes, she wanted
love. But, by breaking the law herself, she was driving
it away from her.

And, if we break a law above the man-made level, we
will always find that we get a direct result. Anyone who
dismisses psychology with the idea that it "excuses ques-
tionable conduct" by giving you a reason why you behave as you do simply does not understand psychology
and its motives. Its aim is to give you a conscious awareness, to explain why these demons exist, so that you may
make a reasoned choice about their disposal.

One woman who came for help finally faced the
thought that she had carried a tremendous hostility for
her mother over into her later life, glared at me and said,
"You know perfectly well that, if I hate my mother, it's
because she made me!" This could be, but it took some
time to show her that, once recognized, there is *no* justi-
fication for continued hostility . . . nor any release for
the one who clings to it.

If I lie, cheat, steal or do any number of conscious
acts that make me feel guilt, this does not indicate a
"psychological quirk" that ought to be removed. This nor-

mal guilt should follow my wrongdoing. A mental pain is a warning just as surely as a pain in the body that all is not well within us. Normal guilt should cause us to adopt those new patterns needed for a healthy soul.

There is this about normal guilt that must be emphasized because of its importance. If I cheat or slander another, for example, I know deep down inside that I am now the kind of a person who can and does do this. The psychologist as well as the religionist calls this "deterioration of character." Unless the deterioration is stopped, or better still, reversed, the toll from this feeling can be deadly.

A college lad came to me recently and told me he had taken a five-dollar bill from his room-mate's wallet while the room-mate was in his shower. He knew his friend would never suspect him, but he was suffering and he wanted my help. "I can't help to relieve you of normal guilt," I explained. "But you can help yourself. Put it back, or, better still, reverse the whole thing with a positive honesty by telling him you did it." He put it back but he was never able to tell and a reserve grew up between him and his friend.

On the other hand, a boy came to me on campus one day and handed me ten dollars. "I owe it to you," he said. "I took tickets for you one night at a play and this stuck to my fingers. I haven't been able to face you since." Since there could be no condemnation in my reaction to a man who was reversing his field, this young man and I became even greater friends than before because I knew the effort and courage that were driving forces in his character.

Normal guilt is a healthy thing. It is one step, however, to the exaggeration of normal guilt where it is all out of proportion. Young men and women "petting" on dates sometimes have agonies of guilt, and guilt regarding normal sexual curiosity in children, or, later, masturbation can become so intense as to court a lifetime sense of guilt or fear of sex. Exaggerated guilt builds morbidity and creates fear.

Some individuals have only "social guilt" feelings. They

feel sure their families or friends would disapprove of what they are doing or would like to do. Carried further, they will hesitate to think these things through, to let their own conscience dictate the answer, but go ahead and do it anyway, because they impulsively want to. This type of person is almost always selfish and self-centered. The gratification is fixed at an infantile level. It is easy for them to rationalize, so they continue to attack and exploit others for their own satisfaction. To them, this spells success. Since people tend to become like the thoughts they hold, these individuals either become degenerate or they grow sick of themselves, bored, suicidal or develop psychosomatic symptoms.

Beyond normal guilt, exaggerated guilt and social guilt, we find still other things that cause us deepest shame which we have pushed down to the non-verbal level where they fester and corrupt. The results are usually devastating. Guilt feelings may cause the disassociation of one function of the body from another so that partial or full impairment results. The field of psychosomatic medicine shows this quite clearly. Our experiments showed it. Examples are numerous.

I have known a minister who was so afraid of his thinking and speaking that his suppressed guilt literally robbed him of the use of his voice. A woman whose husband was an alcoholic developed a form of hysterical blindness when she took his guilt upon herself.

During the war a twenty-four-year-old pilot with whom I flew a mission on Wednesday was hospitalized on Thursday with a useless right arm. It was possible to stick pins in it and there was actually no feeling there. It took some time before this was associated with an episode which happened when he was quite young. In a fit of temper, he hit his smaller sister causing her an injury that impaired her hearing. Under the stress of war this buried guilt which had been driven home by his parents, at length manifested in the disassociation of the offending arm from his bodily functions.

The first step in freeing anyone from this abnormal

guilt is to carry it to the normal, verbal level and have a look at it. Abnormal guilt, then, is the step-sister to the normal conscience. One is destructive. The other constructive. Awareness of this fact will help us recognize the choice we have made between them.

Inferiority Feelings

There is no such thing as a "superiority complex." There is a self-centeredness, self-will. But what appear to be superior attitudes are likely to be a cover for inadequate feelings. It is common knowledge, verified by clinicians and therapists in mental hygiene, that we rate ourselves too low. Why? Partially because of disappointments and frustrations encountered in growing up. Many of us have been ridiculed, humiliated, berated somewhere along the line.

A child is physically and intellectually weak compared with adults, and if the adults he encounters are not motivated by wisdom and love (that unbreakable law), he will endure pressures and frustrations which will make him timid, withdrawing, seclusive. Or he will react in the contrary manner with exhibitionism, rebellion, or almost any type of delinquence. If this difficulty is not resolved in childhood, he will continue to display these infantile reactions.

Katz and Thorpe* link inferiority feelings with an emotional tone of fear. They point out that most of us feel inferior for short periods of time or in certain areas. Inferiority feelings are considered to be a maladjustment of a severe degree only when the attitude of inadequacy becomes associated with nearly all of the experiences of the individual. When this happens, the individual has a feeling of complete inadequacy and unworthiness.

Katz and Thorpe list the following symptoms that would indicate the presence of a rather pronounced degree of inferiority feelings:

---

* *The Psychology of Abnormal Behavior,* by Louis P. Thorpe and Barney Katz, The Ronald Press, 1948.

Seclusiveness: the individual avoids being with other people, refuses to participate in social activities and seeks to be alone.

Self-Consciousness: the individual is reserved and easily upset in the presence of others.

Sensitiveness: the individual is especially sensitive to criticism or unfavorable comparison with other people.

Projection: the individual blames and criticizes others, seeing in them the traits or motives which he feels to be unworthy in himself.

Ideas of Reference: the individual applies to himself all unfavorable remarks as well as criticisms made by others.

Attention-Getting: the individual endeavors to attract attention by any method that seems likely to be successful; he attempts to gain notice by crude devices that are usually not socially rewarding.

Dominating: the individual endeavors to govern others, usually smaller and younger persons, by bullying and brow-beating them.

Compensation: the individual covers up or disguises his inferiority by exaggerating a desirable tendency or trait, sometimes in a socially acceptable manner and sometimes in a socially disapproved (anti-social) one.

A good example of this latter came to one of our later Prayer Therapy classes in the form of a campus wolf. His slips revealed that, while far from feminine, he was not nearly so masculine as he wished to be. For a while he compensated in a socially accepted, if slightly affected manner, contenting himself with a super-masculine walk, manner of speaking and driving all that fulfilled his mental idea of a rugged male. When this proved insufficient to convince himself, he resorted to the less socially acceptable manifestations of "conquest," his conversation and souvenirs were slightly vulgar and supremely unconvincing testimonials to his prowess.

The psychological factors behind this type of inferiority Katz and Thorpe feel to be related to the home environment and, for prevention's sake, we may list the most damaging parental attitudes to the personality as: rejection, unfavorable comparison, teasing, disapproval, severe punishment, and oversolicitude.

Any individual possessing inferiority feelings will undoubtedly attempt to adjust, mostly by withdrawing or by the technique of avoidance. These are the paths most likely taken since there is a constant feeling of embarrassment or of the fear of failure and subsequent ridicule. Excessive day-dreaming and a flight into phantasy become common.

At the childhood level the very first defense against these is *denial*. In the face of a mishap the child says, "I didn't break that, did I, Mother?" This defense or denial does not vanish with childhood. It is carried over into adulthood where it is usually more subtle in its manifestations. With the adult (outside of deliberate lying) this defense by denial now becomes automatic, unconscious, and it is difficult for the adult to recognize what he is actually doing. Therefore he must be made aware of his defense mechanism before he can be honest with himself. These defense mechanisms will be dealt with in detail in Chapter 11.

The chief thing in encouraging people to dare to be honest is to relieve them of the idea that this is a case of deliberate wrongdoing. If stress is laid upon the factors that cause these demons it is to relieve the sense of guilt, the unconscious denial, and allow us to see that much that we think and feel has not been shaped by our own choice but by ideals, prejudices, biases and so forth of our families, friends, neighbors, by customs and standards and traditions which surround us.

Once this is recognized, we are free . . . free to make our own choice and ready for the therapy of prayer.

Misguided Love (Hate)

Nothing deserves more thoughtful consideration in our evaluation of ourselves than our concept of love. It is so important that we will later devote a full chapter to it. Fear, guilt, inferiority feelings revolve around our concept of love, either for ourself or another. The counterpart of love is hate. Strictly speaking, there are only three ways to feel toward another person. We can love them, hate them, or be indifferent toward them. What hate and indifference do to us mentally, physically and spiritually is to keep us partially whole, sick or dying. Hatred has been called "love frustrated," or love misdirected.

The young orange grower who suffered from such deep hostility discerned that "hate is misguided love." He said, "It is the self-same creative energy misdirected, turned destructive."

Mrs. S., the elderly mother-in-law, when she finally came to the point of self-honesty, was amazed at what she found. "My form of Christianity," she said, "had made me self-righteous, blind to my actual motives. If you want to check on that point, see how you honestly feel about God letting His rain fall on the just and the unjust. To be truthful, this has always annoyed me." Once she had learned that such things could happen to a practicing Christian, a "good" woman, she developed two safeguards against a return to her old miseries and fears. It was an old command with a new accent: *"Watch* and pray."

"Through finally accepting my slips," she said, "I found I was infiltrated with a whole fifth column of unwelcome guests. Through prayer I learned to clear them out. But I can only keep my consciousness clear if I am alert to what I don't want and meet it at the gate with wide open eyes." At the approach of an unwelcome, negative emotion, she found she must refuse to rationalize, to excuse. The temptation was to accept *righteous* indignation, *justifiable* anger, *normal* resentment, *helpful* criticism. "That's another way of saying I was trying to build myself up by tearing others down." She had come a long way from complacency and self-righteousness when she could say, "By whatever name you call them, those emotions won't heal the situation and can't fail to leave you personally worse off. Qualifying them soothes you into believing you can misdirect love without harm to yourself if you have a reason, a 'helpful' reason. But it still leaves you tired, spent. And once past your guard and into the unconscious region, it doesn't stay righteous, or justifiable or normal."

The most prevalent attitude that must be surrendered by those who have not yet reached the dangerous zone in misguided love, but are tending in that direction, is our indulgent criticism of others. To realize how common this is we asked a very nice, normal group of women who met regularly for cards to refrain, in their luncheon conversation, from any critical remark, joking or otherwise, about anyone. "What was the result of your attempt?" I asked one of them.

"Self-conscious silence," she said, blushing.

The facets of hate are as many and varied as the facets of love. It is the other side of the coin. Again, one is constructive, one is destructive. The overly critical often find it difficult to forgive others, which is a form of hate. Hate always impoverishes the hater, and most of us recognize this fact, but it wears many disguises which we must tear away.

St. Paul, in a letter to the Romans, beseeches them, "Be ye transformed by the renewing of your mind, that ye may prove what is that good, and acceptable, and perfect, will of God."

Once we have agreed to make prayer a practice in honesty, have taken advantage of the Key, psychology can offer us to show us how to search out the present state of our mind and emotions, we are accepting ourselves as we really are. We can recognize consciously some of our major drives and attitudes. We need not be worried by what we find, whether it is Fear, Guilt, Inferiority or Hate, for now we have a basis for a change, and in the next two chapters a simple, proven method for effecting the "renewal of our minds." But so long as we shirk doing this first job honestly and thoroughly, as long as denial is present within us, no change can take place. If we need further help with this Key, "indication tests" are provided in the chapter "Techniques for Self-Knowledge."

Once we know ourselves as we are today, we are ready to take steps to become what we wish to be tomorrow. We can, if we choose, walk straight toward the kingdom of harmony which is within each and every one of us.

6

THE HEALING POWER

ONE OF THE LEADING PSYCHIATRISTS OF OUR DAY, DR. Karl Menninger, director of the famous Menninger Clinic in Topeka, Kansas, has said, "If we can love enough . . . this is the touchstone. This is the key to the entire therapeutic program of the modern psychiatric hospital. . . . Love is the medicine for the sickness of the world."*

Almost two thousand years ago John, the Beloved Disciple, wrote in a letter, "Perfect love casteth out fear: because fear hath torment. He that feareth is not made perfect in love." We could say that he who has inferiority feelings, abnormal guilt, hate, likewise has not been made perfect in love. From John down through the entire body of literature dedicated to relieving the mind, body, and spirit, unto this day we find the same theme reiterated.

Love is the healing power!

What Is God?

Why is this so? John gave the answer in one of the few definitions we have for God in the entire Bible: *"God is love."* A God of love is our healing power.

Now, there is nothing sensational in this statement.

* *Love Against Hate*, by Karl Menninger, Harcourt, Brace and Co., 1942.

We have all heard it over and over again. We simply do not accept it. If it were to become real to us, an actual part of our consciousness, then we would see miracle upon miracle. But it has been repeated so often that it is almost automatic. Of the countless people whom I have asked to define God, practically everyone has included "God-Is-Love."

But, in our experience in Prayer Therapy as well as with the Random Prayers, we found that, even when they said it, they didn't understand it, feel it, believe it. God, just like Momma and Poppa and Teacher and Santa Claus, would issue a flabby affection if they were good little boys and girls, if they were already perfect (which none of us are). It never occurred to them that we are all, right this minute, as perfect as we are able to be. They brushed aside the Apostle Paul's hard-learned lesson that "the good that I would, I do not: but the evil which I would not, that I do" until, as he put it, "With the mind I myself serve the law of God" (which is Love) and accept "the spirit of adoption whereby we cry, Abba, Father."

Unless we can accept the love of God embracing us now, with all our faults, frailties and shortcomings, we will be no whit better tomorrow than we were today. Unless we can believe in a God of love, we can never learn to be honest. Fear will always stand between us and the healing power. We will find ourselves in the position of the woman who hid all her feelings until she was released by the simple statement that God "knows them anyway and understands." Like Claudia, if we are to accept His help, we must believe in His love. Thus, it was absolutely imperative that our next step be a fearless look at our own concept of God.

In all my experience I have met no one individual who did not believe in a "power greater than myself." I have had them say, "I do not believe in *God*—I believe in 'Nature,' or 'Universal Law,' or 'Creative Intelligence.'" And that is all right, too. There have been sects which called the Supreme Being "Oom" and "Mobile Cosmic

Ether" and, while the latter may be a bit unwieldy for emergency use, there is absolutely none who can say they are wrong. There is no reason at all to shy away from an honest evaluation of what God means to you today. Carl Jung has said, "Whether you call the principle of existence 'God,' 'Matter,' 'Energy' or anything else you like, you have created nothing; you have simply changed a symbol." And this is true. As a matter of fact, we found the student who believed in a Beneficent Power called "Universal Law" was often much closer to a God of Love than one who believed in an "avenging Heavenly Father."

The difficulty we found with the abstract symbol in Prayer Therapy was that, while it would certainly be part of the infinite truth about God, it did us personally little or no good. It was difficult to approach "Universal Law" or "Infinite Energy" with the fact that we could not seem to love our daughter-in-law, or feared our boss, or were a failure at social gatherings. It was well nigh impossible to feel that "Nature" or "Mobile Cosmic Ether" would hear or respond to the burden of guilt, shame, terror or hatred we found plaguing the Kingdom within ourselves.

Yet it was entirely possible to stand before that facet of Infinite Being which Jesus, in His wisdom, called Our Father—an all-powerful, all-good God of Love. Then, without fear, we found we could be honest, open our heart before the healing power, and seek the graces we had need of to reestablish harmony of mind, body, spirit.

This, then, was our second step. It was a necessary outgrowth or complement to the first. In order to *make prayer a practice in honesty,* to search and bring to light all the fear, guilt, hate and inferiority in our mind, we had to *keep our eyes firmly on our concept of the Healing Power—a God of Love.*

Where Is God?

Invariably when we talked of God the individual student located Him someplace . . . far away . . . near at hand . . . up there . . . in the hills whence cometh our help . . . in the church . . . on the altar. And this, too, is true as far as it goes. It simply doesn't go far enough to do us any immediate good. Perhaps we aren't at church or in the hills. And we won't be until next Sunday or next vacation. Again we have a too glib statement: "Well, God is everywhere." And this is also true, as true as the statement that "God is Love." But it won't do us any good until we actually realize that "everywhere" includes us in, as it were. Personalized, the statement "God is everywhere" means "right where I am, God is."

Thus the most wonderful place where we found God, where those of us in Prayer Therapy "located Him" and got to know Him, was in the kingdom within, His kingdom, in our very own mind or consciousness.

It is a completely sterile thing to know God intellectually "out there" or "in heaven" where you have to struggle to reach Him. It is fraught with doubt. Did I get through? Is there really anything to get through *to?* Unless the idea of God can be emotionally felt, unless we can actually experience in some measure the presence of God, everything we have read, heard, or believed will avail us little. We "believe" that which we have been told . . . by someone else. What we have heard or read is also based on someone else's experience, and that someone has benefited. Our benefit comes if we believe what he says sufficiently to open ourselves to a like experience. The discoveries of the orange rancher, Klaus, the wealthy Mrs. V., the elderly mother-in-law in Prayer Therapy were valid encouragement for the rest of us for, as they testified to an inner change, we saw the corresponding outer change. We loved them more as they became more lovable. But nothing altered in *our* lives through *their* change of consciousness. You will not reach the Kingdom of Harmony within yourself on your minister's ticket.

The most dramatic problem offered for solution by Prayer Therapy is a direct testament to, first, the healing power of a God of Love and, second, to the necessity that this concept become a living reality.

The Power of Love vs. the Power of Death

When Clare S. came into the original experiment, she faced the immediate problem of coming to terms with death. Her husband, a veteran of World War II, part owner of a highly successful super-market, had been given twelve months to live, victim of a quick type of cancer from which there was no recorded survival.

On the advice of his physician he had sold his interest in his highly competitive business, taken his family on a long vacation and, on their return, bought a small grocery store where he had direct, leisurely contact with the neighbors whom he served. The idea was to make this last year a great adventure in service, in quiet peace, and the ex-soldier, to whom the face of death was no stranger, was able to accept the challenge. It was his wife, Clare, mother of his two small children, whose growing desperation made unbearable the decreasing time they had together.

When Clare entered our class six of their precious months were gone and she was, as she put it, "losing my mind. After the gay, high-paced life we've lived together for eleven years, I am finding that material values fade in the face of death. I have to find something lasting, something that will withstand death and change, before it is too late!"

Since we were an experimental group, we could give no special handling even in the face of the extremity of her problem. If Prayer Therapy was based on a provable principle, it would effect a sound emotional foundation, a harmony in the Kingdom within. This would be the best protection against the catastrophe of grief pushing her off balance.

Clare had had orthodox religious training and even during the "gay years" had added the respectability of church-going to her varied activities. She belonged to what we called the Christmas-Easter-Sometimes-on-Sunday type of devotee. Her concept of God was vague and undefined . . . a Power someplace in the blue, and now, although she prayed overtime, she got cold comfort. Her prayers were a groping, fumbling effort to make contact with a faraway Stranger.

Following her psychological tests, we gradually let her slips reveal to her the hodge-podge of demons and doubts that haunted her inner world. She had to face them. The burning resentment, the self-pity. . . . "Why did this have to happen to *me*, to *my* husband, to *my* children?" . . . Self-justification. . . . "Why shouldn't I feel resentment, self-pity? If there is a God somewhere, I can't find Him, and He isn't doing a thing for us."

One slip squarely stated that hatred was a mounting force in her consciousness, a sense of retaliation she was fostering against the world. "I don't believe it," she cried. Yet it was true and she eventually came to realize it. On her own investigation she added to this the fact that she had grown irritable, cross and lazy, a sort of "what's the use" attitude based on self-centeredness and misguided love. "I've had to accept myself and stop pretending," she told the class. "I find I am exactly as capable of hating as of loving. A glass can hold the exact same amount of dirty water as pure water. I've let myself be contaminated by resentment."

Were self-pity and resentment the best armor for defense? Was hate a weapon with which to fight the battle of loss? No, she decided. She must attempt to rearm. And the first concrete help she got came with the realization of a God of Love. "It was understanding that Love wasn't a passive ideal," she stated. "Caring is love in action. If I separated God from His activity, I wound up with a comfortless, intellectual abstract. But God *caring,* God manifest, God *doing* meant a flow of creative power lovingly directed . . . Good feelings within me . . . loving reactions . . . Here! Now!"

It was the conviction of the "hereness" . . . the "nowness" of this Creative Love that gave her the emotional experience of His presence. As the experience became more continuous, she began to feel God wherever she was, wherever her husband was, willing and able to care for them both. There was an immediate release from strain in the numbered days of their life together.

In the presence of such Love she was not only healed of resentment, self-pity, but found that hatred had given place to a new kind of joy which she called the "need to worship." "Something within me," she said, "needed to worship and praise God as much as my body needed food and air. I began to feel as though I had starved my . . . well, my soul. I wanted to be *active* in worship, caring for everyone from my husband to the beggar on the street."

In this light, did her concept of death change? "Could I," she asked herself, "keep this wonderful faith if my husband died?" Quietly, simply, convincingly, she gave the class her answer. "I can," she said. "Death is not the important thing. Love is . . . love right this minute. God present right this minute. The moment of death is only another 'this minute' and the minute after that. When I realized God as Love caring this 'now' and found Him in each succeeding 'now,' I had an abiding conviction He would take us through the valley of the shadow or separation, or whatever the instant brought. It has released me from apprehension for the future to live with Him in the 'now.' "

It was a good thing for apprehension had been destroying her by inches, and the moment of parting did not come. Five years have passed and her husband remains very much alive. His last physical checkups have shown no trace of malignancy. Medical authorities do not attempt to explain it and neither do the husband and wife. They were two grateful people and she felt they had both died in a way, to their "old way of looking at things and had been born anew with a whole fresh set of values."

The Commandments of Love

There is the great secret. We *can* be born anew through Love. Love is the healing power and God is love. This is true. Clare proved it. All our Prayer Therapy students proved it to a greater or lesser degree. All we need is love. But we are now at that place where we say,

"Granted. But how do we get more love? Or more loving? How do we experience the Love of God?" It is exactly the same as the sick man who is told that all he needs is health. He will say immediately, "I agree! Help me get health. Show me!"

Fair enough! Unfortunately, love is too little contemplated or too much misunderstood. We stop short at physical love, sentimental love, mother love, or some such facet, and call it a day. Yet, it is our concept of love, our understanding of it today and its unfoldment tomorrow that will govern us. Believe me, the man rotting in jail today is there because of his misunderstanding of love and his consequent misuse of his energies.

His love may have focused on money, possessions, turned sour in jealousy of his wife, run rampant in lust or any one of a hundred variations. Unhappily it was his highest understanding at that moment.

I talked with a young mother in the county jail one day. Drab, listless, pregnant once more, she was not sorry she had killed her tiny daughter. "She cried and cried, and there was no food in the house," she whispered. "I loved her. I loved her." What she needed, what the world needs, what each of us needs is a higher understanding of love. The only difference between the saint at the altar and the sinner in the gutter is the capacity and focus of their love. I repeat . . . the *only* difference. Vital, is it not?

We are a Christian nation. For us Jesus of Nazareth was the most perfect li*ver* and pra*yer* that has come upon the human scene. He lived visibly through the change called death. His prayers were answered with signs following. And He made no secret of His way. He invited us all to come along. How?

Sometimes He spoke in parables, not to confuse but to enlighten. He spoke of everyday things, new patches on old pants, new wine in old bottles, making bread, planting grain—timely and intelligible to the poor and needy and uneducated. The intelligentsia was shut out. It was too simple for them to understand. He spoke to you and to me.

When He gave specific directions about the Way He was absolutely explicit, perfectly straightforward. His whole teaching was based on Love. All four records we have on His life and work are in agreement on that point. He gave us definite things to *do*. What were they? Let us look at His commandments, the only direct commandments that Jesus gave us:

Thou shalt love the Lord thy God with all thy heart, and with all thy soul, and with all thy mind. This is the first and great commandment. And the second is like unto it, Thou shalt love thy neighbor as thyself (Matthew 22:37-39).

The Lord our God is one Lord: And thou shalt love the Lord thy God with all thy heart, and with all thy soul, and with all thy mind, and with all thy strength: this is the first commandment. And the second is like, namely this: Thou shalt love thy neighbor as thyself. There is none other commandment greater than these (Mark 12:30-31).

Luke records it in a conversation with a lawyer who asked Jesus what he must do to inherit eternal life. Jesus asked how he read the spiritual law and the man then answered:

Thou shalt love the Lord thy God with all thy heart, and with all thy soul, and with all thy strength, and with thy mind; and thy neighbor as thyself.

And Jesus said: Thou hast answered right: this do, and thou shalt live (Luke 10:27-28).

John quoted Jesus during His Last Supper with the followers He loved as saying:

A new commandment I give unto you, That ye love one another; as I have loved you, that ye also love one another (John 13:34).

Again:

"This is my commandment, that ye love one another as I have loved you" (John 15:12).

When He was going to His crucifixion, the greatest proof of His love, wherein He laid down His earthly life to give us the proof and reassurance of Eternal Life, He made one last appeal to His students: "If ye love me, *keep* my commandments."

Now Jesus stressed the fact that His commandments were not separate. The one was "like unto" the other. Together they formed a positive circle, just as we found the four demons formed a negative circle. As we could enter the latter at various points for purposes of eviction, so we can enter the circle of His commandments in several ways. The point is that we will not be made perfect until the circle is complete.

This symbol of the unbroken curve is a familiar one. One thing leads to another, we say. Emerson in his essay on Circles writes: "The eye is the first circle; the horizon which it forms the second; and throughout nature this primary figure is repeated without end. It is the highest emblem in the cipher of the world. St. Augustine described the nature of God as a circle whose center is everywhere and its circumference nowhere."

Jesus told us that this Circle was Love.

In our Prayer Therapy Experiment we observed four points at which the circle could be entered and found that, once entered at any point, the completion was inevitable, a matter of time, governed only by the force of individual need or desire and the rapidity of growth in our understanding of prayer, an art which we will discuss fully in a later chapter.

Jesus' Circle of Love as taught in His commandments represents in equal importance love of God, of neighbor, and of self. When these are pure and complete we will find ourselves pure and complete, triumphant, victorious, without demons to disturb, made perfect and whole physically and mentally. Then the most important question is where do we begin? How can we "get more loving"?

7

ENTERING THE WINNER'S CIRCLE

ALL THOSE WHO HAVE WON THROUGH TO A LASTING victory over their problems have found a way to penetrate the Circle of Love. The first successful approach observed by our Prayer Therapy Group seemed to be outwardly passive, a matter of deep inner need or desire. It is necessary to point out here that in our experience no one approach appeared more virtuous nor more effective than another. All led to the same completion and the choice of entry depended simply on the emotional content and aptitude of the individual seeking admission.

The First Approach—The Hound of Heaven

This initial passive route hinged chiefly on an ability to comprehend emotionally, to *feel* John's words: "We love him because he first loved us."

Clare was a prime example of this. Her need was deep, urgent, emotional, and this was answered by a powerful and overwhelming conviction that God actively, here and now, loved her, her husband, the beggar on the street. She was into the Circle for, at this point, she began at once to fulfill the first requisite of Jesus' instruction by answering this love. Her experience was loving God with her whole heart, mind, soul, strength. She was then able to accept (love) herself just as she

was. If God loved her with all her shortcomings, she
could be honest, look at them without fear or evasion.
Love for Him bred within her a desire for greater perfection and mind and energy cooperated with grace to
throw off hatred, resentment and the rest.

This is a feeling we all understand. Why do we wish
to be wiser, more successful, more attractive? What spurs
us on to attempt greater things? Love . . . usually for
family, child, sweetheart . . . rarely is it self-love, the desire to please ourselves alone. Thus we can follow Clare
in her desire to match her love for God with greater
purity.

A second fruit was the need to worship and to worship in action, in service, in active caring . . . her neighbor as well as her husband . . . and her concept of
neighbor altered to include all God's children, even the
beggar on the street. In a short time she had at least
touched the outer rim of the Circle . . . loved God, herself, and her neighbor as herself.

Justice Oliver Wendell Holmes once said that his
whole religion could be summed up in two words: "Our
Father." This, as Clare discovered, is an entire prayer in
itself. If we meditate upon it, we see why. A God of
Love, Father, Creator, Sustainer of self and neighbor
and every living thing, wraps the whole world in the
Unity of Love, One Father, One Brotherhood.

But the opening into this mystery came to Clare with
the realization that "Our Father" loved *her*.

This was also true in the case of a young man afflicted
since childhood with an agonizing stutter. When he entered Prayer Therapy, Tony's tests revealed tremendous
insecurity and inferiority feelings. Although he attended
class regularly and faithfully, attempted to follow his
homework by releasing these things before God, for
some months he made little progress. Suddenly we
sensed a change in him. Within a matter of weeks his
speech clarified. "What happened?" the class asked.

"Well," Tony explained, "at the beginning of the experiment you remember I could sing without a hesita-

tion but I couldn't speak. I thought 'Brahms wrote that song. I wrote me.' Then a couple of weeks ago after my morning prayer time, I had a sudden conviction that God wrote both Brahms and me. If God valued me enough to create me, He loved me. *God* loved *me!*" With this came a feeling of exultation, a loss of his sense of inferiority and his reluctance to express himself.

The physical cure here was gratifying but it was only one fruit. The wonderful thing was that he had sought and found God, touched the Heavenly Kingdom within and, just as Jesus had promised, outer things began being added. His speech healing was only one of many. Entrance into Love's Circle led him, as it had Clare, to a singing love of God, thence to a reevaluation of himself as God's child. He could love and have confidence in a personality sired by a Heavenly Father. His unfoldment had begun.

This same was true of Tina, the lady with the philandering husband. First she had to be convinced that her business was not to change *him.* All any of us has to work with, in the last analysis, is ourself. As Tina began to accept Our Father as all Love, she was able to evaluate the Self God had intended her to be. As she became more nearly like that Self, she sensed that the love she expressed toward her neighbor (her husband included) should be returned, and it was. Here, again, healing of the asthmatic condition was simply an inevitable fruit of the healing within. Her woman friends said that Tina had at least learned to hold her head up. That was true. But we in Prayer Therapy knew why it was true and how she had learned.

This, then, was the first method of entering the Circle wherein a loving God was the initiator, the actor, the pursuer and the students were simply open through deep desire and the consciousness of their need to the experience of God's love for them. The Hound of Heaven, as the poet, Francis Thompson, clearly saw, can in our dire need break through and set its love to dispel our cares and burdens.

The Second Approach—"I Love Because I Love"

This method was used effectively by only one member of the class but it is well worth recording if a single reader should thereby find his individual Way to a realization of Love. Our ineffectual minister, Rev. G., entered the circle of love by loving God. It is a paradox to say that his difficulties all stemmed from the fact that he loved Him not, that he doubted and feared Him, distrusted the salvation he was recommending to his flock, and that he overcame this by loving Him.

Yet that is precisely what happened. Rev. G. desired above all things to believe in, to trust, to love God. When he realized that he had been kidding himself, he took that to God in prayer, and asked to be helped to love Him, to know Him. Innumerable times a day he reminded his conscious mind that he *did* love Him, *did* believe and trust, and his subconscious acted upon this repeated suggestion. It responded to his deep desires from the hidden storehouse where it is always one with the law of love precisely as the body of the spastic Dr. Carlson was brought under its control when his deep desires penetrated to it during a delicate surgical operation.

This idea of suggestion and the cooperation of the subconscious will be gone into in more detail in our chapter on prayer. It is enough to say here that fulfilling the commandments of Love can begin with a deep desire to love God and the conscious endeavor to do so.

This is not a new idea and its execution was fascinatingly detailed in a conversation recorded by Jean Pierre Camus, the young Bishop of Belley, when he sought directions of his beloved master, Francis de Sales.

"I once asked the Bishop of Geneva what one must do to attain perfection. 'You must love God with all your heart,' he answered, 'and your neighbor as yourself.' I did not ask wherein perfection lies, I rejoined, but how to attain it. 'Charity,' he said again, 'that is both the means and the end, and the only way by which we can reach that perfection which is, after all, but Charity itself . . . just as the soul is the life of the body, so charity is the life of the soul.'

"I know all that, I said. But I want to know *how* one is to love God with all one's heart and one's neighbor as oneself.

"But again he answered, 'We must love God with all our hearts and our neighbor as ourselves.'

"I am no further along than I was, I replied. Tell me how to acquire such love."

" 'The best way, the shortest and easiest way of loving God with all one's heart is to love Him wholly and heartily!'

"He would give no other answer. At last, however, the Bishop said, 'There are many besides you who want me to tell them of secret ways of becoming perfect and I can only tell them that the sole secret is a hearty love of God, and the only way of attaining that love is by loving. You learn to speak by speaking, to study by studying, to run by running, to work by working; and just so you learn to love God and man by loving. Begin as a mere apprentice and the very power of love will lead you on to become a master of the art. Those who have made most progress will continually press on, never believing themselves to have reached their end; for charity should go on increasing until we draw our last breath.' "

Both this approach, learning to love by loving, and the first, opening to the experience of the love of God for the individual, are internal routes, their roots in strong already present emotional desires, and deal primarily with the first commandment—to love God and then the neighbor and self. In the other two approaches we found successful for us, the initial accent was on the second commandment, to love thy neighbor as thyself, and was active, external, with the internal experience following.

The Third Approach—Starting in Our Own Front Yard

Let us go back to the mother-in-law whose major demons were variations on hate. We remember that her private slips, the result of her early tests, pointed forcefully to a lack of outgoing love particularly toward her daughter-in-law. Her first response toward the uncovering of such un-Christian motives and drives within herself was to be angry and insulted but, with the challenge of self-honesty, she was forced to admit first to herself and later to the group that much of her personal unhappiness would dissolve if she could have a more loving reaction toward those around her.

The class in general discussion evolved a simple yardstick, three qualities which they felt would appear as the fruit of love: loyalty, self-sacrifice, forgiveness. By this yardstick her relationship to others did not measure up. She never missed a chance to criticize, although she cloaked it in the Christian term "rebuke." Sacrifice she believed pointedly and patiently should come to her and not from her. Nor could she forgive the smallest mistake in others which she could invert to bolster her self-esteem. In truth, she had fallen into the common trap of letting the fulness of years breed fear and inferiority, the ghost of uselessness and loneliness, specters which we found that Prayer Therapy could dispel.

For Mrs. S. the first step after honestly recognizing this need and trying to form a concept of a God of Love came when she started to apply the yardstick to her daily thoughts and actions. "I couldn't love on order," she said, "but I could pray to be made more loving and then act as if this prayer had been granted." She began measuring her reactions to her daughter-in-law. Loyalty forced her to discontinue discussing her with others. Self-sacrifice set her looking for small things to do and, if discovered to her personal glory, she would refuse to count them. Some of these sacrifices, though small, were difficult and against the grain. She would refuse cheerfully to accept invitations which her son felt obliged to issue because "mother is lonely" but which she knew, from her own happily married days, were expeditions for two. She tried to sacrifice her personal feelings even when weariness, grouchiness, bodily discomfort tempted her to complain for sympathy, and present a cheerful face. She forgave by "releasing, giving over" any shortcomings she noticed in others to God.

The wonder was that these conscious, willful acts of love, which were in the beginning at variance with her true feelings, became genuine responses. She had believed when she joined us that what she needed was more prayer power to change other people's lives. Instead she found love changing her life and everyone around her reflecting that change. It is an inevitable result of the law that love reflects love. Before class was over her daughter-in-law had driven down to Redlands with her, to join for a day in the class that had "worked miracles for Mother S." Mother S.'s body, even to the arthritis which had given her so much trouble when the experiment began, testified that release from those subtle emotional poisons could set it free to function normally and naturally, that it had been succumbing not to old age but to the stresses and strains which her mind had imposed upon it.

Most of us can begin at once to act as if our prayerful request to love had been granted. But it is absolutely vital that we remember Jesus' qualification that we are to love others *as ourselves*. Remember that we did truly find in Prayer Therapy that most of us rate ourselves too low and that, as we showed in the last chapter, the majority of our fear, guilt, inferiority and hate stem from this. It would be dangerous indeed to fasten this concept of ourselves on others and yet that is precisely what we do. To follow His command we must begin by being as kind to ourselves as we would be to others . . . to forgive ourselves before we can forgive them.

This is no lesson in arrogance but it is designed to show that Jesus recognized that self-condemnation is not humility. Over and over He forgave sick people, lifted their burden of guilt and condemnation. "Son, thy sins are forgiven thee," and a healing took place.

The children of God do not crawl on the face of the earth! They walk upright. They were given dominion. Dominion was given to you and me, a gift, by Grace, from a loving Creator. Then let us dare to take it, to fulfill His purpose by exercising this dominion over ourselves, over our environment, *but* let us be humble. If, in our true Self, all errors stripped away, we are "a little lower than the angels, crowned with glory and honor," if we are "joint heirs with Christ to all the heavenly riches," it is not of our doing.

Let us *give God the credit. Look to Him* as the *Source.* Then surely the laws of love will govern our dominion. Then we can never fall into the pit of personal pride, or into the ditch on the other side of claiming God made us miserable worms. In Prayer Therapy we found this our compass for walking safely on the straight path of loving ourselves without conceit. This was our definition of humility.

Give God the credit.

Since this approach of loving one's neighbor as oneself is the gateway most easily accessible to all of us, and since we had found our understanding of love to be the force that dictated the course of our lives, our experimental group spent a good deal of class time enlarging our concept. We gained a great deal from a sermon preached almost sixty years ago by a Scottish minister, Henry Drummond, to a band of youthful missionaries. He took for his text St. Paul's magnificent message on Love in the thirteenth chapter of 1st Corinthians. So much truth was wrapped in Drummond's interpretation of what he called "The Greatest Thing in the World" that his words describing the Supreme Good have lived on and on in one pamphlet after another.

Drummond said, "In those days (the days of Paul) men were working their passage to heaven by keeping the Ten Commandments, and the hundred and ten they had manufactured out of them. Christ said, I will show you a more simple way. If you love, you will unconsciously fulfill the whole law."

St. Augustine had the same thought in mind when he set down his formula: "Love, and do what you like."

In the seventeenth century John Everard, a spiritually minded divine plunged into the midst of revolution, military dictatorship, a materialistic clergy, tried to persuade the people that this alone was the road to world peace: "Turn the man loose," he wrote, "who has found the living Guide within him, and then let him neglect the outward if he can! Just as you would say to a man who loves his wife with all tenderness, 'You are at liberty to beat her, hurt her, kill her, if you want to.'"

The law of love for God, self, and neighbor as set down by Jesus would supercede the need for any other law from the superficial traffic law to the moral laws of Moses. If this seems strange, think on it a moment.

Drummond points out that "if man loved man . . . it would be preposterous to tell him not to kill. You could only insult him if you suggested that he should not steal . . . it would be superfluous to beg him not to bear false witness against his neighbor. If he loved him it would be the last thing he would do. And you would never dream of urging him not to covet what his neighbor had. He would rather they possessed it than himself. In this way, 'Love is the fulfilling of the law.' It is the rule for fulfilling all rules, the new commandment for keeping all the old commandments, Christ's one secret of the Christian life."

In short, love could usher in the millennium, heaven on earth, peace and good will, security, individual happiness . . . love bringing us to the Kingdom of Heaven within and all these things added.

St. Paul passed love through a prism and Henry Drummond lists these component parts and interprets them as the nine ingredients of the Spectrum of Love:

Patience—"Love suffereth long"
Kindness—"And is kind"
Generosity—"Love envieth not"
Humility—"Love vaunteth not itself, is not puffed up"
    (Gives God the credit)
Courtesy—"Doth not behave itself unseemly"
Unselfishness—"Seeketh not her own"
Good Temper—"Is not easily provoked"
Guileness—"Thinketh no evil"
Sincerity—"Rejoiceth not in iniquity, but rejoiceth in the truth"

These, says Drummond, make up the Supreme Gift, the stature of the perfect man. He continues, "You will observe that all are in relation to men, in relation to life, in relation to the known today and the near tomorrow, and not to the unknown eternity. We hear much of love to God; Christ spoke much of love to man. We make a great deal of peace with heaven; Christ made much of peace on earth." Again there is a priority for Hereness, Nowness, rather than a wishful casting of our hopes toward the further side of eternity.

Here, then, is the third starting point from which we entered love's circle, the active way of commencing now to practice love toward neighbor and self. These simple virtues we have always known don't look so difficult: patience, kindness, generosity, humility, courtesy, unselfishness, good temper, guilelessness, sincerity, but added together, they fulfill and suffuse our actions and character with brotherly love. And this simple beginning can lead us around the full circle until we receive the full benefit of love's healing power.

The Fourth Approach—Angels in Disguise

The secret of the fourth way to begin to understand and enter into Love is revealed in a single line by Dr. Leslie Weatherhead.*

"Love, even the love of God, is only mediated through persons."

Hasn't this already been our experience even if we have failed to notice it? Love, which is God, has been mediated to us through parents, teachers, husbands, wives, friends, physicians, the stranger within the gates. This love was mediated personally. Impersonal love has touched us too, through artists and composers, inventors, scientists who have worked years to develop vaccines,

* *Psychology, Religion and Healing,* by Leslie D. Weatherhead, Abingdon-Cokesbury Press, 1951.

public servants, statesmen and the like. But we must be aware of it to reap any spiritual benefit.

Our first introduction to love came to us through the nine aforementioned ingredients being expressed toward us in an ascending or descending scale. Where love was misguided, we have been hurt. Where it was Divinely directed we have been helped, comforted, healed, inspired, sometimes even raised by another's faith and love to heights we never suspected within ourselves.

At its highest we touch the secret and pierce the mystery of the saving Grace experienced by many as the Christ-love personalized by Jesus. Sometimes this comes through an awareness of the sacrificial love He must have felt toward all of us which led Him on the way of the Cross, that His resurrection might give us proof of Eternal Life. Sometimes it comes through belief in the healing balm of His promises: "Come unto me, all ye that labour and are heavy laden, and I will give you rest . . . Let not your hearts be troubled. . . . Continue ye in my love . . . Lo, I am with you always, even unto the end of the world."

Our first dim awareness of Divine love mediated through persons may come to us at our mother's breast, or with our first experience of tenderness, forgiveness, understanding. If we recognize it as an answering warmth, gratitude, appreciation, thanksgiving dawns in us until love reaching toward us touches an answering chord and we *love because we are loved*.

Klaus, the epileptic in the Prayer Therapy experiment, a man who honestly thought he was an atheist, whom medicine and psychology considered hopeless, gained his first awareness of love, the healing power, when he was felled by an epileptic seizure before the entire class. When he came to himself, his companions were not shrinking from him, not condemning him or shunning him. Instead we remember he found that the entire group had stood by him and prayed earnestly for his speedy recovery.

The opening of the circle to Klaus was to find love mediated through his fellow man. This he could see. This he could believe. With this tiny grain of faith in love expressed toward him by a handful of students, he went on to his complete healing.

I was discussing our experiments one day with a talented young actress whose conversion experience some years ago is well known in Hollywood. I told her about Klaus and her face lit up with a smile of sympathetic understanding.

"Klaus is my spiritual brother," she said. "I, too, had a problem with atheism, alcohol, a scandal which made me hostile, resentful, insecure. For a year I resisted the attempts of . . . (she mentioned a famous woman motion picture star), who was a close friend, to get me to a young people's chapel group. Finally I went. I took my bottle with me. I was defiant, waiting for someone to cast the first stone."

She hesitated and seemed to fight down a lump in her throat. "Nobody did," she said simply. "Instead, those kids, whose Master was Jesus, loved me . . . me . . . just as I was, a pretty miserable specimen. No questions asked. They prayed for me . . . for *me!* I found out later they had been praying for me for a year. What did I do? What could I do? I loved 'em back. I wanted to get rid of all my excess baggage (her demons) and have Christ for my Saviour too!"

There was the opening, love mediated first through the friend, then through the group, through the figure of Christ to bring a stray sheep back to shelter, security and usefulness. But here we have a very important point, another circle proceeding from the original. As Emerson put it: "Our life is an apprenticeship to the truth, that around every circle another circle must be drawn." As we accept the love directed toward us, we are responsible for its continuation, its circulation, and we thus join hands with the Saviour to become the mediator of love outward again to our fellow man.

We dare not shun this responsibility.

We can remember here the haunting story of the discouraged young man who started for the river to commit suicide. His landlady, suspecting his intent and conscious of several weeks' rent owing her, tried to dissuade him. "I'll tell you," he said. "If I meet just one person between here and the river who gives me a smile, or a word of hope, or a look of cheer, I'll be back. Life will seem worth living." He never came back and the landlady didn't know what the outcome was. But what if he had passed us that day?

We truly begin to see that we must love, or take the consequences.

Love, by whatever method we discover it, produces a new outlook, a new set of values, rebirth, a new way of life. In its dramatic and instantaneous form we have the genuine conversion experience, always accompanied by some degree of healing whether physical, moral, mental, or emotional. Greed, lust, envy, drunkenness, hatred, guilt, all manner of errors fade in this sudden full light.

For most of us, however, this experience is a slower process, and it requires conscious effort on our part. It requires deep desire and prayer. But is this not worth our best effort, when we know conclusively that our God of Love is our healing power?

One more point should be held firmly in our consciousness. *There is no limit to the Power of Love . . .* nothing too large, nothing too small, nothing too difficult, nothing unworthy of this healing, cleansing, creative energy.

The Healing of Nations

The leaves of the tree of life, according to the Revelations of St. John the Divine, are for the "healing of nations." Love and life are one. We could never have one without the other for there would be no reproduction of the species, no care or provision for the young, no curb whatsoever on the dog-eat-dog instincts that every so often threaten to depopulate the earth. Now nations, like individuals, have their demons and the healing power and method is the same.

Lest this seem a wild statement in these times, a dreamer whistling in the face of the A-Bomb, let us look at the proof. During our own century we have seen one man lead a nation out of bondage to another nation without his army firing a shot, taxing the population for arms, but using as its single weapon the highest form of love which the united soul of the masses could achieve.

Mahatma Gandhi was not a military but a spiritual genius, and he led India to freedom from British rule by love.

The Mahatma was a Hindu saint but his friend and biographer, Louis Fischer, tells of visiting him for a week and finding "only one decoration on the mud walls of his hut: a black and white print of Jesus with the inscription, 'He Is Our Peace.'"* Mr. Fischer asked Gandhi about it and the Mahatma replied, "I am a Christian, and a Hindu, and a Moslem, and a Jew." This is what we might call Universal Love and while few of us can hope to attain it, we must never be too narrow to admire it when it flashes across our horizons.

The American missionary, Dr. E. Stanley Jones, who knew Gandhi intimately for years, said of him: "One of the most Christlike men in history was not called a Christian at all," yet observing his life and works he thought, "God uses many instruments, and he may have used Mahatma Gandhi to help Christianize unchristian Christianity." For while the Hindu leader loved Jesus, violence in any form contradicted his understanding of the Sermon on the Mount and the Commandments of Love. He took Christ more literally than many of those who use his name and was, Mr. Fischer wrote, "addicted to love; it was the basis of his relationship with people. Love is creative interdependence."

The non-violence upon which Gandhi based his successful struggle for Indian independence was, according to Fischer, "more than peacefulness or pacifism; it (was) love, and excluded evil thought, undue haste, lies or hatred." For Gandhi you could not gloss demons with syrup or sentiment. They had to be honestly rooted out. As with our individual Prayer Therapy students, his

* *The Life of Mahatma Gandhi,* by Louis Fischer, Harper & Brothers, 1950.

first step was an honest evaluation of the national consciousness. He found Moslem-Hindu disunity (based on fear, hatred, intolerance), Child Marriages (a circle of demons), Untouchability (segregation as we would call it, another circle of guilt, fear, inferiority, hatred) which must be brought to light and overcome before his beloved country could respect (love) itself. Only then would it be strong enough to practice "Satyagraha" which means truth-force or love-force, the non-violent kind of battle which was to set them free.

The exciting story of exactly how this worked has unhappily no place in our pages but we find heartening confirmation and proof that when this pattern was followed it did free and heal a nation as surely as it healed and freed the individual. Had Gandhi continued to lead India we can only speculate on the place he might have taken in world events.

Fischer makes one further comment on Gandhi which is pertinent to us here. "Gandhi's relation with God was part of a triangle which included his fellow man. On this triangle he based his system of ethics and morality." We have called it a circle. Louis Fischer calls it a triangle. And how did this "Christlike" man view God, the pinnacle of the triangle?

As that which was permanent, unchangeable, immortal, Gandhi once wrote, "In the midst of death life persists, in the midst of untruth truth persists, in the midst of darkness light persists. Hence I gather that God is Life, Truth, and Love. He is Love. He is the supreme Good."

Jesus Christ, John the Beloved Disciple, the Hindu Saint, the Scotch minister, Dr. Karl Menninger, . . . all agreed on the Supreme Good. And our Prayer Therapy students found that what was true for saint and expert, true two thousand years ago and thousands of miles away, was true for you and me. Here! Now!

There was nothing new in our intuitive need for a concept of God as Love, the omnipotent, omnipresent Healing Power, before whom we could dare to make our prayers a practice in honesty. All the testimony we could

find pointed up the urgency of entering the Circle of
Love offered by Christ which must be completed before we could be "made perfect." Thus an important
part of our Prayer Therapy experiment was the tested
methods by which we found we could contact this limitless Power, begin to get more love, be more loving, and
ultimately experience the active, healing, guiding Love of
the living God. Briefly, once more, here they are:

ONE: We can open ourselves through prayer and
meditation to the direct experience of God's love
for us. "We love him because he first loved us."

TWO: We can "begin as mere apprentices" and by
deep desire, prayer and conscious will insist that we
do now love God with mind, heart, soul, and strength
knowing that "the very power of love will lead us on
to become masters in the art."

THREE: We can use the yardstick of Loyalty, Self-
Sacrifice, Forgiveness to measure our present relationship to ourselves and our neighbors, prayerfully
ask that the nine ingredients of love filter through
our every thought and deed, and then *act as if this
were so.*

FOUR: We can observe with gratitude, appreciation, thanksgiving, the love mediated to us by child,
friend, relative, stranger, public servant, teacher, and
follow this mediation to its peak of perfection in
Jesus and great spiritual leaders until an answering
love floods our being and we eagerly pray to become
worthy channels through which this inspiration may
pass to others.

It does not matter where we begin. We may have confidence from the first instant that we make a conscious effort to keep the commandments that our victory, our salvation is assured. Lest this word mean exclusively a future
state to some it should be pointed out that Salvation, in
truth, means "safe return." Here and now, once we em-
bark on the path of love, our "safe return" to the Kingdom of Heaven within, and all the added things—peace,
harmony, joy—are in our grasp.

8

HOW TO CAST OUT DEMONS

WHEN ROBERT LOUIS STEVENSON WAS FOUR YEARS OLD he announced a great discovery. "Mamma," he said, "you cannot be good without praying."

"How do you know?" his mother asked.

"Because," said he, "I have tried."

In Prayer Therapy we found there was almost as much truth as humor in his simple statement. The principal means we found for effecting a change within ourselves was through prayer. It was through prayer that we could loose our demons and let them go. In each of the four approaches to the Circle of Love prayer was a prime requisite. The reason was obvious.

A God of Love was our inspiration and our healing power. And *Prayer was our means of communication with God.*

Here we were abruptly faced with the fact that, while prayer had been tried by most of us for years and years in some form, and by mankind for century upon century, neither the individuals nor the world seemed to manifest any great degree of change or improvement. It would appear that young Stevenson's maxim could be inverted. It was very possible to pray without getting any better.

Teach Us to Pray—with Signs Following

Yet the lives of the enlightened, from the humble ones who have mastered the art to the great saints, have indicated that this should not be so. Our Prayer Therapy experiment proved that, if we started humbly asking, as did the disciples, "Teach us to pray," the way opened up to the rank and file.

Each and every one of us could learn to pray—with signs following. We need not "pray amiss."

That a great deal of energy could be expended in the name of prayer without successful results was borne out by our Random Pray*ers*. Some of their errors have already been uncovered for us in the past three chapters. As Joshua Liebman emphasized again and again, "They would have peace of mind but will not look within."

They had been either too ignorant or too fearful to make their prayers a practice in honesty and, had they wished to do so, they had no cognizance of the four demons, no guide to search out their true drives. As a substitute for actual honesty there was the tendency toward blanket self-condemnation, a low, wormy evaluation of self which made it extremely dangerous to evaluate their neighbor in the selfsame way. Their concept of God was a capricious, far-off, unpredictable Being or a consistently just-wrathful-vengeful Parent who did nothing to help their admitted backsliding.

Their prayers were negative. Their results were negative.

If we have been praying and praying and *praying* without getting anywhere we must be quick to see that there is nothing here which condemns us. We may have suffered from the error precisely as we suffer from an error in our bank reckoning. But there is no sin involved. Our communications have been faulty. The lines are tangled or down.

If we have not been praying at all, then no attempt at communication has been made. Again there is no condemnation. Possibly we didn't understand the principle or the need. Possibly we just didn't believe in it. A friend of my grandmother's who lived in a rural area for a long time did not "believe" in the telephone. For her, while the rest of the world got the benefit of this new form of communication, it did not exist. She wrote letters to folks in the town and waited patiently for answers. She sent her husband driving through the night for the veterinary. Then she visited my grandmother and saw the reality of the telephone. Immediately she had one installed and it worked just as well for her as for grandma who had been one of the pioneer telephone owners. Grandma's friend came in at the 11th hour but, exactly as the laborers in the vineyard, she was not penalized for a late start. She received full value because the principle was constant, ever available and no respecter of persons.

So we found it to be with the principles of prayer. They are constant, ever available, and no respecter of persons. It did not matter if the pray*er* had been praying amiss for 2 years, or had never prayed before. It was only necessary to know how to use the telephone once it was installed and recognized as a valuable form of communication. The instrument itself availed nothing.

Once the principles of prayer are understood our lines of communication are established. It remains only for us to use it. Now, how did we, in Prayer Therapy, establish this all important communication with God? Our experiments showed us that there were four points inherent in successful prayer: we had to pray regularly, make prayer an act of surrender and honesty, make it positive, and make it receptive.

Make Prayer a Regular Activity

Let us say right here that our class found most writings on prayer made it sound too easy. It isn't. Those who use it as a spare tire, only when an emergency arises, are very apt to be disappointed in its results.

At one time the sculptor, Rodin, was approached by an extremely enthusiastic tourist who had viewed his major works in Paris. "Oh, Mr. Rodin," she fluttered. "Is it difficult to sculpt?"

"Not at all, Madam," replied the master. "You simply buy a block of marble and chip away what you don't want." Simple? Yes! Easy? No!

Each of us must realize that, within our own block of marble, imprisoned by the fogs of our own making that hem us in and stand between us and our true Self, stands the Son of God, just as surely as the magnificent statues of Rodin were already complete both within his material and in the mind of the sculptor. The process then is one of freeing this Self which was made in the image and likeness of God. This will not be accomplished overnight for the reason that our prayer techniques will not be perfected overnight. Demons, doubts, unwanted bits and pieces must be chipped away, sacrificed gladly to Love's healing power through prayer as soon as recognized, until we stand free.

Prayer is simple, yes, but it is no easy art . . . except sometimes for little children who are completely trusting. For most of us this most rewarding skill, as with all others, will never be mastered on a hit or miss basis. *Prayer must be made a regular and regulative part of life.*

In one of our classes we had a young lawyer who had developed an ulcer. He was an Irishman, attractive, mercurial, and a great problem to himself. Within there was constant friction between a native belligerence and a need to be admired and loved. On the one hand he wanted all to react to the charm he had squeezed from the Blarney stone and on the other, in the words of the old Irish Bull, "he was never at peace unless he was fighting."

His mind was facile and his tongue glib, natural talents for a courtroom counsel, and in a few short weeks he announced that he "had" Prayer Therapy, honesty, demons, God of Love, 4 points of prayer—and he did too. On the very tip of his tongue. Physically he felt much better and we saw him no more.

The difficulty was that what he had on the tip of his tongue, what his quick intellect had mastered so easily had not penetrated to his heart (or emotions, to use the psychological term). Prayer had become neither a regular nor a regulative part of his life and his mastery of it deserted him almost as quickly as it had come. A year later he was back, his ulcer condition aggravated, his increased suffering having opened his way to see that he had missed this first vital point entirely.

We must be patient with ourselves if we would master prayer. Dedication and deep desire reinforce our will and carry us through arid periods when prayer does not come easily and we had rather not. If we are tempted to abandon regular prayer in moments when we are feeling fine, or conversely, when inspiration is lacking and we feel we have no talent for it, we can recall the little girl who fell out of bed during the night.

Her mother heard the crash, rushed in alarmed and picked her up crooning sympathy. "I'm all right, Mommy," said the child. "I just fell asleep too close to where I got in."

We must pray regularly not only to develop skill but so that it becomes a regulative part of our lives and we do not fall asleep too close to where we got in. No psychiatrist or psychologist or any other therapist would expect a patient to be helped if he came to the clinic irregularly or only a few times. Very probably he would dismiss the patient. There is a follow through, a gradual unfoldment, in all therapeutics.

Regular prayer helps one to identify oneself gradually with the spirit of Love—the spirit of Christ—the mind that was in Christ Jesus. It establishes internal controls which begin to give us spontaneously the responses we need. For this reason we must bring as much sincerity as we now possess to our prayers.

By praying regularly the last thing at night before retiring, and the first thing in the morning, always with an emphasis on Love, our prayer power will begin to increase measurably. Even in our present imperfect condition, still in the "presence of our enemies"—our doubts and demons, we will find we are growing toward that most Holy state which Brother Lawrence called the "practice of the Presence of God."

Said Fenelon: "Do not be discouraged at your faults; bear with yourself in correcting them, as you would with your neighbor. Accustom yourself gradually to carry prayer into all your daily occupations. Speak, move, work in peace, as if you were in prayer."

When we can achieve consistency in this we will find

ourselves being freed of our demons, dwelling in more abundant life, tasting the peace that passeth understanding.

Make Prayer an Act of Surrender

The original Prayer Therapy group dubbed this act of surrender "praying dangerously." Surrender sounds so passive, so spineless—and they found it quite the reverse. "To surrender everything," said Klaus, "that is to take the biggest dare of all."

The theory behind complete surrender is a well known one to the physical sciences. Nature abhors a vacuum, in fact will not tolerate one. Something always rushes in to fill the seeming emptiness.

Now, what would happen if we could manage, by true surrender, holding nothing back, to create a vacuum and invite God to fill the void? "Surrender-your-life-to-God-thy-Will-not-Mine-be-done" is almost as overworked as a religious phrase as "God-is-everywhere-God-is-Love." It is also nearly as little understood. The point is that we are to practice as well as admire this grand statement. If we stop to look at it we find it presupposes a God you can trust—One already there waiting to fill the vacuum lovingly, with Good. Faith then is a must for adequate or complete surrender. When we have seen this accomplished in individual lives we have seen miracles.

Dr. Norman Vincent Peale has shared the story of his first moment of complete surrender with us . . . and we have all been witnesses to its outcome. The same act has been part and parcel of others who have had great spiritual impact upon our life and times: Peter Marshall, Sam Shoemaker, Harry Emerson Fosdick, Mary Baker Eddy, Albert Schweitzer, Bishop Fulton Sheen, Billy Graham, Martin Buber, Abraham Joshua Heschel, each and every one, regardless of separate theology, has testified to and proved the need of surrender—Thy Will Be Done.

But we think of them as somehow apart from ordinary sinning, suffering humanity. We say to ourselves, "Faith is already theirs—and purity. They are merely offering

up a well-polished vessel for higher purposes." The point
is that we will not attain any higher unless we will surrender the limitations of today to make way for fresh
thoughts, inspirations, goals, and understanding. That is
how they advanced. It is how we will advance. If we fall
short of their perfect faith, we must begin right where
we are with our grain of hope or bit of trust. Faith is not
like gasoline, in danger of running out if we go too far.
It is more like a muscle which strengthens and grows from
practice and use.

To surrender now, this minute, we not only offer the
vehicle of our lives, our virtues, talents, will, but our burdens and demons as well. These latter will dissolve in
proportion to our willingness to be made whole.

Most of us think we are already willing to be made
whole. But are we?

A woman of forty, a housewife and mother, entered
Prayer Therapy when her physicians as well as her spiritual advisor had given up all hope of helping her to overcome alcoholism. She wanted desperately to stop drinking, was carrying a load of guilt, fear, shame that had
driven her twice to unsuccessful attempts to end her life.
Her slips revealed deep-seated resentments, tremendous
self-pity, guilt, inferiority, a staggering burden separating
her from any awareness of Love's healing power. Deeply
religious, she could not understand why her prayers to
stop drinking had not been answered. At first she showed
little interest in eliminating the detrimental personality
aspects uncovered to her.

"I want to stop drinking first," she repeated. "If I can't
stop *that,* what does it matter? Why doesn't God help
me?"

God couldn't help her because she wouldn't let Him.
She was *not* willing to let go—and let God. She began to
realize this when we studied a healing recorded in St.
John which contained a puzzling question by Jesus. He
asked a man who had been infirm for thirty-eight years,
"Wilt thou be made whole?"

Now, as we have agreed, almost everyone suffering to
any degree believes they are willing to be made whole.

Still Jesus must have had something specific in mind. Isn't what most of us want to be healthy, or free of pain, or free of debt, just as the one thing our alcoholic wanted was to stop drinking?

When the purpose of Jesus' question dawned on her she found that, in her heart of hearts, she had *not* been willing to be made whole—only sober. She wished the pain of drink (only a symptom in reality) removed whilst she clung to her resentments, her self-pity, her guilts and so forth. This cannot be.

We must be *willing* to surrender everything.

The human personality is a dual personality. Within each of us there is an infantile portion and an adult portion. Since this is true it is foolish to say to ourselves or others, "Grow up." Saying this will not make it so. Jesus as well as modern psychology says, "Become new." Becoming new is not always as easy as we have been led to believe. Our learning has come about by conditioning. Conditioning is learning but that doesn't mean it is necessarily all good. Unless a person is psychotic, the ego within each of us has the upper hand. This often makes it difficult for us to surrender our detrimental feelings and attitudes. We have to learn to surrender ourselves—our whole world of inner feeling—to a Spirit greater than our own. "Spirit of God descend upon my heart!"

True prayer means releasing ourselves under the compulsion of the highest, not in dreary resignation, but in joy and trust. Again, until faith is adequate we can begin right where we are and pour forth our problems, our shortcomings, our desires and dreams as best we can before a God of Love enthroned *within us,* inviting Him to fill the void, take over our lives, remove our shortcomings, to direct, guard and guide.

This is to become *willing* to be made whole. It is not a matter of human will power, aggressive insistence, frenzied begging, but rather a relaxed, gentle, trustful release of all our burdens to a Power greater than ourselves.

By this act we stop regarding influence, power and causation as arising from outside. We begin to realize that essentially the power for good or evil comes from within.

Our inner thoughts may not actually change the world (for very possibly the world doesn't need changing except as individuals change) but they will certainly change *our* world for *us*. Here we must look one step ahead and guard against the danger of accepting surrender as a sort of illusory state in which we do nothing. A change will not come for us if we only think other thoughts. Faith must eventually be matched over against action. Our new thoughts must lead to new deeds.

What new deeds must we do? First, we must stop blaming other people and outer conditions and adopt a dynamic attitude toward life. We can stop treating others as if they were responsible for the present condition of our development. What may have been done was done through ignorance, therefore all blame will cease. With this new attitude there will be no time for regret and we can turn up a new path immediately and start afresh.

The woman alcoholic learned that it was not the fact that her life was limited and mean, that her husband earned insufficiently to grant all the things she desired, that her children were more troublesome than other people's children, which brought on her drinking bouts. Her condition resulted from the fact that her attitude toward life was limited and mean. Her relationship to her husband and children was resentful, frustrated, lacking in love. It was only as she faced these attitudes, became willing to surrender them and to match her actions against the yardstick of loyalty, Self-sacrifice, Forgiveness that the healing power could be released in her life and that life could be changed for her. This is exactly what happened.

When we turn within in an act of surrender we find that law and order are here. Guidance is here. All life is ready. We must see that we are reaping as we have sown and that we may sow and reap anew. Was it lack of love on our part? Was it meanness? Was it selfishness? Was it a lost opportunity that left us bitter and resentful? It matters little what the particular experience may have been. By becoming aware of the detrimental aspects within, by being willing to let them go completely, we will broadcast new seed and escape the harvest of more inferiority, fear, guilt, hatred that have distorted our view of life. It is a Law: The Universe will give back action for action. Nothing could be plainer than this.

We surrender, then, our old selves, our old way of thought and action. We release ourselves under the compulsion of the highest. Unless we do, we suffer. The only value of suffering (and we have seen that it is created through our own ignorance or misuse of impersonal laws and not imposed by God) is that when it becomes sufficient it may at length force us to an honest evaluation. For some the pain threshold is high, for some low. But when we have had all that we can bear, we will then turn with a willingness to be made whole. At this point we will dare to surrender our old selves, turn totally and trustingly to our Healing Power of love and guidance. Now the eviction process has begun and we are being made new.

Make Prayer Positive

Our surrender has created a void. How can we be sure it will not fill up again with the same murky thoughts and fears that we found were habitual to us?

The specific answer lies in positive prayer.

We found the Random Prayers using negative prayer, that is holding their unhappy symptoms directly in the focus of their attention. Over and over they declared they were unhappy, suffering, sinful and unworthy. Though these affirmations of misery were addressed to Our Father still nothing, absolutely nothing, happened to contradict them. They went right on being unhappy, ill, sinful just as they held they were. Why? Because even God cannot break His own laws. God's laws are like His nature and one with them—constant, dependable, without flaw or variation.

Here we are dealing with the most misunderstood point about answered prayer. Our prayers are *always* answered! We found there was no mistake about that.

"As a man thinketh in his heart, so is he. . . . It is done unto us as we believe. . . . When ye pray believe that ye have received and ye shall receive. . . ." But *what are we praying?* What are we repeating and believing constantly either on our knees before the altar or going about our daily business?

Earlier we said we need not fear wrong thoughts unless they got our attention . . . that we could brush them aside and refuse them and they would have no power. Well, let's reverse this. Suppose we say the Lord's Prayer, which is a positive, affirmative prayer, once a day. But it doesn't get our attention. We brush it aside and go right back to telling God what a thorough failure, what an unhappy specimen we are and continue dwelling on these thoughts during our waking hours. What is getting our attention? It is not the brief moment with the Lord's Prayer then that is *our* prayer. Our constant thoughts and words of affirmation are *our* prayer, that which will have power in *our* lives. Thus, "You are what you pray" whether you ever pray consciously or not. We may even create a vacuum through a successful and complete act of surrender but then, if we turn and dwell on self-pity, self-doubt, weakness, guilt, fear, pain, do we honestly believe we have let God's will for His creation dictate our state of mind?

Believe me, we saw definite proof that our prayers are answered *in kind*. We all of us, atheist, agnostic, religionist, believe that if we plant a poppy seed that seed will grow by the law of Nature into a poppy. That is a law as dependable as the rising and setting of the sun. Never once has a man planted a poppy seed and gotten a cabbage. It is exactly the same with prayer and the law is as exact and irrefutable.

Negative prayer will produce negative results. It is ridiculous to blame either God or prayer power. Neither has let us down. Quite the contrary. For it is by the selfsame law that positive prayer will produce positive results exactly as the same law by which a piece of iron sinks will cause a battleship to float. We must simply understand that law and use it correctly.

To understand the law of positive prayer we must look once more at our important ally, the subconscious. Now the subconscious is not something separate and apart from us. It is a part of the Kingdom within, and a most important part. It has always been there and it has always been functioning, whether we make conscious use of it or not. It is not something new invented by psychology. Psychology has simply given some study and a label to that which has always been within our make-up, always reacting to the stimuli we offered it. It is the slave of the conditioned mind—for besides doing its own work of keeping in order those functions with which the conscious has no concern but regards as automatic, the subconscious also serves the conscious by producing from an infinite storehouse according to the pattern we offer it. Here is free choice and dominion indeed!

When Dr. Carlson's deep desire demanded that he be steady while he performed a delicate surgical operation the subconscious was the go-between and the body responded. When Rev. G. affirmed his present ability to know and understand and trust God, once more there was a response in kind. When Esther, in the Random Prayer group, insisted that the world was evil, that she would wait for improvement hereafter, and declared constantly that she was depressed and despondent, her outlook remained unchanged and so did her world. Her subconscious had no choice but to obey.

Here is a force which is impartial, impersonal, without moral sense or discrimination and has no alternative but to follow our dictates whether these be a steady diet of fear, anxiety, suffering, limitation or healthy happy aims and concepts. But it is always producing *something,* of that we may be sure. And we, either knowingly or unknowingly, are placing our orders this minute for each unfolding minute and taking delivery. In this sense the future does belong to us, to make it anything we wish.

To the degree that we understand this we become successful pray*ers* and masters of our own destiny.

Bill, a man who entered the Prayer Therapy class on a doctor's recommendation, had conquered alcohol only to break forth with attacks of "pseudo" or non-organic epilepsy. He never succeeded in pinning his violent hatreds or resentments on any individual. "I hated constantly but impartially," he said, "the world at large."

Honestly striving for a concept of a God of Love he had to be willing to surrender that attitude and then quickly change his mental diet. To reverse his direction he decided he must picture himself as vigorously loving the world at large. His mind could only learn by constant repetition, he said, as had been proven when he struggled with the multiplication tables and the alphabet. "Broke, discredited, wizened and mean, I could not remake myself overnight. But in class we had agreed to start where we were so I began to fancy myself as a kind of beloved vagabond." Stray cats, dogs, other derelicts were his first target but as this positive concept became more habitual the subconscious responded and Bill became more and more lovable and less and less vagabond. By the time he was offered a position as foreman in a foundry he was, indeed, a very popular fellow.

In class he became a great favorite for his vivid way of making his smallest experiments come alive, as with his application of positive prayer to a painful, expensive siege at the dentist.

"I've saved enough to get my teeth fixed," he announced one day. "I've always had a resentment against a guy who gets rich yanking my teeth and making jokes while he's got me helpless. I've had a sneaky fear of him too since I was a kid. So for years I haven't gone. He hasn't missed me but you should see my teeth."

He decided that before his first appointment he had better surrender his resentments and fears, for the last session he could dimly remember had been very stormy. He would pray positively, regularly, every time he thought of the coming event, and see himself as calm, serene, poised and unafraid.

"So," he reported after the first visit, "I'm sitting in the dentist chair and the oddest thoughts keep coming to me. I think, this dentist, if he just wants to get rich he could sure find an easier way than looking down my throat. He's a good dentist, too, so he must be sort of dedicated, must love his work and indirectly my new bridge. So in a way he loves me, incisors, biscuspids and all. Well, there isn't a single harmful element in love. Why does he make jokes? Maybe he's trying to make my visit pleasant—must be tough being a dentist and regarded as a necessary evil. I should laugh at his jokes, maybe.

"We're getting along fine and out comes the novocain. I find I'm thinking about the guy who perfected the stuff. Nice of him. Hundreds of thousands of people must be grateful to this guy even if they don't know his name.

"I think—'Gratitude is a fruit of love just like criticism is a fruit of resentment.' That's a good thought and I go over it so I'll remember it."

"Suddenly three teeth are out! I haven't thought about myself once. The dentist and I are filled with admiration for each other. I have *been* serene, calm, poised—exactly as I pictured myself."

He accepted a little good natured kidding from a woman who hadn't "got" the idea of positive prayer yet. "Pollyanna? Auto-suggestion?" Bill shrugged. "I wouldn't know. My education stopped short of that stuff. And maybe I'm glad. Anyhow, I didn't wind up like the last time, throwing a fit or going out for gin. I'm like the ex-blind guy in the Bible when the bright boys of his day were trying to pin him down. He just insisted, 'This one thing I know. Whereas I was blind, now I see.'"

In our positive prayer we regarded our affirmative statements as promptings of God meant to sink into and become a part of our whole being. As Bill had discovered, it was difficult, if not impossible, for any change to take place without mental imagery. With the mind's eye we must see ourselves as we desire to be. As we constantly hold this image and re-emphasize it, we tend to become like the mental image we hold. Through positive imagery our life can become one continual unfoldment. The unfoldment will be in proportion to the integrity of one's personality and not from set words and phrases.

We found prayer by affirmation more powerful than prayer by petition for two obvious reasons. It placed the answering medium within and not afar off, and it offered food to the subconscious. Remember, the subconscious is not the dictating Power but the law answering the power precisely as electricity is governed by an infallible law which the dictating intelligence can require to produce light, or power the electric chair. Our Word is the Intelligence dictating to the subconscious which responds by impersonal, infallible law. Our positive prayer puts us on the side of God's will, bringing from the invisible to the visible in our individual lives that which is Holy —or whole, wholesome, as that word truly means.

If we hold guilt, fear, hate, in our conscious mind, the subconscious will react accordingly. If we simply shove it out of conscious sight but still retain the thought or emotion, it can still dictate without our full conscious co-operation and knowledge. Thus honesty and surrender are imperative. If, on the other hand, we hold Faith, Hope, Love in the center of our attention the subconscious will act upon these. Can we doubt that these are in line with God's will? Jesus said that the Father told him what he should tell us and that his "commandment is everlasting life." And the instructions to everlasting life were, we remember, the Commandments of Love. So we cannot doubt that the will of God in us is the Way of Love and everlasting life. The word of God, then, in our prayers will be positive, affirmative, loving. In one form or another we will reiterate that "He made everything that was made and found it good, very good." As He goes on creating and recreating in and through us, through this Word of truth, it will still be good, very good, in our personal experience unless we ourselves limit, block or pervert it by a mental act.

Growth is the fundamental law of life, so we plant the positive, helpful creative thoughts which cannot help but grow for they have the force of the Universe behind them. At the same instant we see ourselves the way we wish to be in our mind's eye. If we expect failure, we will get failure. If we expect a little, we will get a little.

Prayer, someone said, is a cup held up to be filled. What is the size and shape of our cup? We ask—and we receive. But we dictate the form as we ask.

Thus in Prayer Therapy we tried to fill our minds with great, loving, positive reading, a study on which to draw our blueprints for asking, a means of enlarging and stirring our imagination. We turned in many directions —to the Psalms, Isaiah, the New Testament, the works of enlightened men and women through the ages—and we found the material positive, uplifting, healing in its concept. By reading, study and prayer we focus the mind positively, affirming what we desire. Not by force but by faith does the subconscious become our ally.

Make Prayer Receptive

We come now to the final point without which we found prayer of any nature ineffectual.

Suppose a member of our family, or a beloved friend, came to us hungry and asking for bread—or even roast beef—and we had a limitless supply. Undoubtedly we would give it to them. But that would not be the end of the matter. It would be the end so far as we were concerned. We could do no more.

Still the act is not complete. To do any good the hungry one must take it and eat it. If he fails to act, refuses to receive, loaf after loaf could fall to the floor without his need being met even though we went on offering the supply indefinitely.

This sounds farfetched. It isn't.

Over and over in the beginning of our experiment we found that we did not know how to receive, and, in many cases, did not even expect to receive. Our Random Prayers confirmed for us that, unless we could and would accept the desired good, the act of prayer remained incomplete.

A case in point was Jerry, the minister's son, who continued to ask forgiveness for a certain past act each evening. Since he never gave up begging for it, even though he approached his faroff God with a contrite heart and the act had never been repeated, he obviously either did not believe God could or would forgive him or he simply did not take the forgiveness.

It *is* done unto us as we believe.

Jerry continued to bear his burden of guilt. He did not *let* Love's forgiveness dissolve it.

Why is it so hard for us to take forgiveness? In Prayer Therapy we meditated on the line in the Lord's Prayer: "Forgive us our debts as we forgive our debtors." Jesus had a definite reason for including that precisely as he had a reason for everything else he taught. The obvious one here was a restatement of the Golden Rule—to do unto others what we wish done unto us. We found a deeper meaning as well. Too many of us, instead of accepting man in God's image, have envisioned God in man's image. Since we are prone to hold grudges, ill will, contempt, in short to withhold the fulness of love, God in man's image would tend to do the same. For some of us the first step toward believing we can receive forgiveness is to find that we can give it.

This step has only to do with our ability to accept. Grudges and the like, while they may be temporarily manifested by finite man, cannot be true of Infinite Love. God is not man. Although His spark of Life, Wisdom and Love is within us all, His ways are higher than our ways, His thoughts than our thoughts, as the prophet Isaiah emphatically told us. It is very annoying to be told that "it isn't necessary for us to know the exact way in which a seemingly insurmountable problem can be worked out, since the solution lies with God, and all things are possible to Him." The reason we are annoyed is because we fear the answer may be withheld, or come too late. But this is never the fact unless we insist upon it. Again we are limiting God to human patterns. God is all power, faithful and true, withholding no good thing. He is Love—all of a piece. Robert Ingersoll truly said: "An honest God is the noblest work of man," and an absolute necessity to successful prayer.

When, then, we regularly take our true desires to God, surrendering all that does not check with the law of love, positively affirming our good as in line with His will, there is yet one thing missing. "When ye pray, believe that ye have received and ye shall receive."

The final act of completed prayer is to receive (accept the desired good and act from the knowledge that it is now so).

A woman in one of our classes had a definite problem in her family relationships. She was highly nervous, irritable, confused to the point where each day found her far behind in her appointed duties, straining and panting after peace. "We live in Bedlam," she complained time and again. "I don't know if it's my fault, my husband's, the boys', or dear old Auntie's (Auntie was a permanent non-paying guest), but somebody is always out of step."

She had faithfully tried to practice our Prayer Therapy unfoldments, acknowledged her demons, developed her concept of an ever present God of Love. She prayed regularly, surrendered, affirmed. Still Mrs. R.'s situation quite frankly did not improve. She was a "Yes-But" type of prayer. She deliberately limited God's effectiveness by denying the possibility that He could do the whole job.

Here was the situation. Her true desires were in line with love—a harmonious family. But every time she stated this, her immediate reaction was that, do what *she* would about it, Papa, or Larry, or Bruce, or Joe, or Auntie, would prove too much for Almighty God just as they did for her. Here we have the basic reason why problems involving human relations always seem the most difficult to overcome. To the human sense, to our limited human effort and ability to plan, the ultimate result appears to depend on the conduct and individuality of others. And it is true that we, ourselves, cannot change others by coercion. Free will in the other fellow is a law we cannot buck. Yet the God within us is also the Spirit within them and the power of prayer to evolve a harmonious unity or whole works on the same principle for many as for one. What blesses one must bless all if it is to be in line with the law of love and harmony.

The difficulty comes precisely where Mrs. R. had

found it. She was trying by mental imagery and affirmation to free herself while still holding the others involved in bondage to a declaration of inharmony. She denied the possibility that all things could work together for good and saw her family as obstructing and destroying the pattern of harmony. Because she failed to accept the good she desired she could not treat them, as Goethe says, as if they were what they ought to be, thereby making it possible for them to fulfill the improved concept. She could not seem to release her habitual mental image of chaos until harmony was the accomplished fact. She wanted the cart before the horse for we knew by this time that God and the things of God, such as harmony, peace, poise, power, work from the invisible to the visible and not vice versa.

It would be completely misleading to say that we can make this reversal a part of our conscious mind and belief just by reading that it is so, any more than we can immediately and completely reverse our habitual thought patterns from negative to positive. By conditioning we believe what we see. Actually most of us regard electricity as a fact because we see the lamp glow and the vacuum cleaner run. But the man who can harness electricity believes and understands the invisible laws and principles by which it operates and can therefore with complete faith avail himself of that power and force to do what his *mind and imagination dictate*. When he draws his plans on paper he accepts the power of electricity as capable of fulfilling those plans before he can see the finished results. The idea comes first. If it is in line with the principle it will manifest from the invisible to the visible. So learning to accept the power of prayer as capable of producing the thing desired requires conscious study to understand the principle and the effort to prove it. In the beginning we may accept someone else's word as a basis for our own experiments precisely as does the man who uses the laws of electricity. It is not necessary for him to go back and *discover* it, fly a kite in an electrical storm, and so on.

Since the time of Jesus we have had a clear statement

of the laws which govern successful prayer. It was through studying his instructions that Mrs. R. found the missing piece in her application of that law to her family situation. In class we reviewed two Bible stories, one of which dealt with Jesus' healing of a woman "diseased twelve years" and the other with a blind beggar on the highway. The woman had touched his garment, her way of asking, "for she believed within herself, if I may but touch his clothes, I shall be whole." *Immediately,* the story relates, she was healed. Likewise, the blind beggar, Bartimeus, asked to receive his sight. "And *immediately* his eyes received sight." In both instances Jesus announced that not he, but their faith, had made them whole.

We were studying these in connection with the rule we developed that no detrimental personality aspect or demon should receive our direct attention in prayer for longer than one week. Should we persist in one phase we were blocking ourselves by denying that we had received our answer. It would be comparable to planting the poppy seed and then doubting the law which operated to fulfill its growth by poking a worried finger in the earth to make sure it was still there, or digging it up to see if it had rooted and was growing. Once planted we would give our prayer seed care, positive light and refreshment by our affirmative consciousness; we would pull up any weeds that tried to choke it, but we would let the seed fulfill itself.

Like the sick woman and Bartimeus, we were to ask believing and know that our faith had been answered. No "buts" about it.

"It was the single word 'immediately' that helped me," Mrs. R. said. "I decided that, when I asked in faith for a better family relationship, it must be 'immediately' so, even if I could not see it for the moment. As long as I worried, fretted, kept looking for signs, I in truth hadn't accepted the new situation. I denied my own affirmation and God's power. So I decided to let it go—let it grow— and give it time to manifest before my eyes. And to give thanks that *it was so*. I would be happy about it. Go my way rejoicing."

Was the healing of the whole situation visible immediately? No. However, when she heard angry or hostile words from members of her household she refused to begin to doubt again, but simply recalled that she had asked for a good thing in good faith and it was *so!* She said she would weed out contradictory thoughts by holding this antidote in the center of her attention: "It is so now—since it is in line with the will of love and I have asked and affirmed it. I have received my answer. I thank God for my harmonious household." Then by every outward word and deed she cooperated with that already established internal peace so that it might become visible for all to clearly see. The affirmative picture which she now fully accepted within her own consciousness did become manifest without.

Over and over we proved that whatever we had need of, whether it was harmony, forgiveness, courage, abundance, friendship, health, if we would affirm it and accept it within it would become a part of our outward experience. This was both the secret and the miracle.

We found a second facet not to be overlooked in receptive prayer. While accepting changed attitudes and changed conditions, we could go a step farther. In receptive prayer inspiration, guidance, creative ideas, the correct solution to apparent problems, all were awaiting us within. We had but to heed the ancient wisdom of a tribe of American Indians: "Listen, or thy tongue will keep thee deaf."

Communication with God had to be *two-way* communication if we were to receive the full benefit. No matter how affirmative the approach we would not get full value if we were arrested at the stage of the spiritual chatterbox. If we wanted deeper answers, increased awareness, continuous unfoldment and growth we had to open our consciousness and listen. True, our answers came as thoughts, feelings, impulses, intuitions. We found God's responses natural and normal and never in a single case a startling psychic manifestation. This listening prayer in no wise contradicts our affirmative prayer but crowns it with inspiration and the sense of Presence and victory. Our affirmations can follow a higher good as Divine inspiration leads us on to uplifted vision.

In a sense it is comparable to the man who had been viewing some of the more colorful canvases of the American artist, Turner. When he chanced to meet the painter he said critically, "*I* never see any sunsets like yours." Turner regarded him for a moment and replied, "Don't you wish you could?"

If we wish we could see more of beauty, enlarge our concept of wisdom, love, we must develop an inner receptivity. At this stage in our prayer life the Prayer Therapy Group agreed that contemplative, listening prayer was no easy skill to develop in our complex, busy lives, and that its practice would take some "selling." Emerson helped "sell" us on the need for this final step when he wrote: "What we commonly call man, the eating, drinking, planting, counting man, does not, as we know him, represent himself but misrepresents himself. Him we do not respect, but the soul, whose organ he is, would he let it appear through his actions, would make our knees bend. When it breathes through his intellect, it is genius; when it breathes through his will, it is virtue; when it flows through his affections, it is love."

How are we to become the organs of this soul, this Godliness within ourselves, unless we will be still and know that it is there, unless we listen and permit its impulse to breathe through our actions, our intellect, will, affections? What we *do* is the answer to the inspiration we *receive* from within. We have been studying methods for clearing the lines of communication, of positively identifying our everyday world-weary self with this Self. Should we stop short of listening to God on the other end of the line? We found we agreed wholeheartedly with Pamela Grey who said: "For one soul that exclaims, 'Speak, Lord, for thy servant heareth,' there are ten that say, 'Hear, Lord! For thy servant speaketh,' and there is no rest for these."

9

THE SIGNS FOLLOWING

NOW SIGNS WERE TO FOLLOW THEM THAT BELIEVED, according to Jesus. If our four points together totaled successful prayer, scientifically these signs should be evident and repeatable. They should prove themselves an effective means of casting out guilt, inferiority, fear, hate, and setting us free of the mental chains that have held us in bondage to discordant conditions. You will remember that this is precisely what the results of the original experiment indicated and what five years of subsequent Prayer Therapy groups confirmed.

Let us see, in two typical cases, exactly how this worked.

We are already familiar with the young orange rancher who entered the original experiment when a well-known clinic had recommended surgery for acute stomach ulcer. We followed him through the first step, making prayer a practice in honesty, know that he identified inferiority, guilt, fear, hate as driving forces in his personality make-up. We remember that he glimpsed love when he recognized this hostility as "the selfsame creative energy misdirected, turned destructive." At this point he had discovered what he actually was, what he did not wish to be—and was ready to do something about it.

Precisely what did he do?

In a letter he wrote recently he stated he worked for quite a while on his concept of a God of Love for he found it was not easy to stand before the throne of Grace and mentally uncover his shortcomings. "Don't think," he wrote, "that it doesn't take courage to say to the Boss, 'I hate my mother, or my neighbor or my fifth-cousin-twice-removed,' because you know it's strictly against the rules."

He finally entered the Circle of Love by the third method charted: using the yardstick of Loyalty, Self-Sacrifice, Forgiveness to measure the present relations between his neighbors and himself, then prayerfully asked that Love should filter through his every thought, word and deed.

"After that," he reported, "I was ready for the act of surrender. Trying to fulfill the law of love made it possible to pour out all the things I didn't want in my life before God, always with the idea that I was really offering Him a vacuum to infill.

"Regularly, each night and morning, I would follow my surrender with positive concepts of myself as I wished to be, as I felt He meant me to be. When I felt I had received the thing I affirmed—forgiveness, guidance, inspiration—I could let guilt go."

As he daily and positively turned the direction of his energies over to God he became convinced they were being used for creative purposes. "That took care of inferiority. If I could grow a fine orange I was a part of life, necessary to the Divine Plan. I was needed, wanted. As part of a Divine Plan I had nothing to fear. I would be sustained for service. Without fear I could stop collecting my neighbors' weakness as potential ammunition should they attack me or let me down. Hostility was pointless. I quit being an armed fortress, let the walls crumble, and stood free."

Simple? Yes. Easy? No! It can be briefed in half a dozen paragraphs. It was not accomplished in half an hour. Only after twenty-three weeks did his ulcers disappear, but disappear they did, although he emphasized that he had abided by the Prayer Therapy rule of never praying about his symptoms. However, losing his ulcers did not end his practice of Prayer Therapy. "To this day," he concluded, "I am still applying Prayer Therapy in my daily life. If I am going to set God's man free from my block of marble I can't stop with chipping away a couple of ulcers and a hunk of guilt, fear, and hostility. Finding God as a present, ever available Creative Power you want to go on until nothing stands between Him and His image imprisoned within yourself. When that happens, I should say we would enter an even more wonderful phase of living."

He Knows It, Anyhow

I also asked Claudia R. to set down exactly how she applied Prayer Therapy to overcome the "emotional immaturity, tensions, fears, excessive guilt" indicated by her slips. It was Claudia, with her intellectual brilliance, great personal charm, her devout religious nature, who had carried from childhood the determination to bury everything that wasn't "good" about herself where none, least of all her Heavenly Father, should suspect it until the fears and guilts suppressed beneath a rigid control were manifesting as sciatica, migraine, low blood pressure and the like. For a while, as we have recorded, she made little progress until she received the slip upon which we had penciled: "Don't be afraid to talk it over with God. He knows it anyhow—and understands."

"With that," Claudia wrote, "the whole dam burst. So —I was tortured by a fear of people, felt unsure, inferior, sometimes wanted to be mean and spiteful—or was attacked by jealousy, anger, hurt feelings, suspicion. There! It was *out*. God knew it anyway so I could admit it. Admitting it I was ready to make a change. At first there were times when I had to argue with myself so I wouldn't go into prayer with my 'good girl' face, all decked out in personal glory, and hide the hurts and confusions and difficulties. But I'd remind myself that, since His kingdom was within me, of course He knew the truth. And since he was Love—of course He'd understand.

"Where formerly I had used prayer to gloss over and suppress my feelings I now used it as a means of freeing myself. Every morning I took these definite steps:

1.   Concentrated—centered my mind.

2.   Meditated on a God of Love and my relationship to Him.

3.   Asked to be sustained so I could be made more usable to Love's plan, approach His work without this crushing load.

4.   Released the load verbally—feelings of insecurity, incompetence, anger, anything on my slip for the week plus anything else that was bothering me.

5.   Affirmed that I was now free and as God meant me to be—then stayed silent until I had a strong feeling of victory and serenity. (If tempted to bustle off to other business I'd ask myself 'Have you anything more important to do?')

6.   Went forth expecting—sure that I had received."

(We can note here that Claudia's prayer pattern followed the four points—was regular, positive, an act of surrender, and receptive.)

"My strong tendency toward hurt feelings responded to a suggestion made in class that we try to *delay our responses* on the spot and insist on the reaction we wanted. For instance, I'd go into the bank. Mr. Jones would be brusk, rude. All right, I am hurt. But I have come to understand that hurt feelings are symptomatic of inferiority, insecurity. So I question my reaction. Why am I hurt? He makes me feel small, insecure. Ah, but I don't measure my security by what he can do for me. *God* gives me all. Mr. Jones' manners probably have nothing to do with me. Maybe he has a problem of his own. Then I bless him. Bless his problem. God gives *him* all, too. 'But' . . . says the old habitual reaction. 'No buts' I insist. 'I am strong, joyous, secure. So is Mr. Jones. Where we are, God is. I stand on this.'

"I can positively state that, if we try daily to choose our reactions, the right one will finally become automatic, just as everything else does with practice. We have to make a conscious act of it in the beginning but when it has been adopted as a pattern by the subconscious it becomes a reflex or instinctive response exactly as the act of driving a car becomes instinctive. When this happens physical complaints as well as human relationships, released from the strain of inner conflict, fall into normal, healthy patterns—the *natural* pattern—God's will.

"As you know, before the experiment ended in June of 1952 sciatica, migraine, jitters, all the rest had disappeared. My husband swears I have had better health and better temper than any time since he has known me and that goes back practically to my youth. Yet I work harder, longer (and more willingly) as I approach my 50th birthday. I still apply Prayer Therapy daily since I've no wish to lose all I've gained. Perhaps the biggest thing to me is that I can approach each day, all people and situations with undimmed joy and enthusiasm. And that, for the first time in my memory, I don't wish to be somebody else. I am actually enjoying being *me*."

These then are concrete examples of how we learned to change our direction and walk in serenity, physical well being, with sound mind and purpose toward personal fulfillment. Here, with a minimum of froth and eloquence, is the method we proved could effect the "renewing of our minds": First, a knowledge that the Kingdom within was indeed the kingdom of cause while outer conditions were the effects, and varied according to what governed our consciousness: then a Key to honest evaluation of what ruled in our individual consciousness: acknowledgment of any guilt, hate, inferiority or fear which was dictating to our subconscious and manifesting in bodily or day-to-day inharmonies. We then recognized a God of Love within us as the ever-present, ever-willing, and ever-able Healing Power which could cast out all demons. We began to fulfill the Commandments of Love and used a four-point technique in prayer which would put us in constant communication with our Healing and Directing Power.

The type of prayer for which we make such bold and life-saving claims had to be Regular, an Act of Surrender, Positive and Receptive. This type of prayer did eliminate our detrimental personality aspects and leave us free to function according to that "good, and acceptable, and perfect will of God" which is life everlasting, perfection, and the peace which passeth understanding.

We found this method dependable and repeatable, which academically and scientifically indicate an underlying principle. We proved that prayer does work just as surely today as two thousand years ago, and so anyone who is willing to make the effort can change their direction and follow this path toward more abundant life.

10

FURTHER EXPERIMENTS

THE ORIGINAL EXPERIMENT ENDED IN JUNE OF 1952. In following years we dropped the control groups which had served their purpose but carried on and expanded our work. Results from our subsequent groups have been equally good, sometimes surpassing the percentage improvements noted with the original fifteen Prayer Therapy students. While it was impossible for us to admit all the volunteer "guinea pigs," since we were still dedicated to the academic work of testing, proving and improving and had to limit our experiments to a workable number, we did expand to a hundred individuals which has given us a wider field of proof.

Some of our later results are worth noting.

That the entire family could benefit from the application of Prayer Therapy by a single member was established in the 1952 and 1953 general experiments. Five mothers of children receiving help at the Speech and Hearing clinic asked to study Prayer Therapy. Their children made giant strides beyond the others as Mama's emotional conflicts were resolved and Father was the first to claim an all round improvement at home.

One such mother coined a phrase. "There is nothing the matter with that child of mine," she said, "except that he has been 'spiritually wounded.'" This was true, for, in my experience, children suffering from functional, nonorganic disorders have indeed been "spiritually wounded" by direct fear, hate, or something lacking of a spiritual quality in the home.

In 1953, in addition to the regular group, thirty-two Redlands University students, juniors and seniors from ages nineteen to twenty-two, formed two separate classes to study Prayer Therapy under the leadership of Jim E. Parker. Jim was not a personal relation but a twenty-six-year-old ordained American Baptist minister who had done postgraduate work as a student therapist with the original project. We already knew that the medical world and the field of education alone could not immunize young people against destructive emotional forces. We wanted to see if prayer could.

Far from attracting campus misfits, these student classes included the year's student body president, the girl elected head of the Associated Women Students, the president of the inter-fraternity council, six athletic stars as well as nine psychology majors, four pre-ministerial students, three teachers-to-be, a "wolf," an agnostic and an atheist.

"We were 98 per cent ordinary, normal people," one of the football players stated in a report. "But each of us received help from Prayer Therapy." A leading fraternity man summed up, "Besides providing us a housecleaning method and some new values for 'now,' what we learned should go a long way toward preventing conflicts and emotional blow-ups in the future."

Frankly I was amazed when these voluntary classes with no recruiting system beyond word of mouth, offering no credits, absorbing valuable time, had to turn students away. It is too early to evaluate the long term effects of Prayer Therapy as an immunizing agent. But a most hopeful indication that it could have the desired result was in the measurable and visible changes it wrought in one short year.

Here we are dealing with a student group, the fortunate per cent of our future citizens who are able to acquire "higher learning," and we discovered what psychology has long suspected—that intellectual education does *not* educate the whole man. In fact it often barely touches the emotional side of his nature, leaving it to toddle along in immaturity actually dictating in many ways to the more carefully nurtured intellect.

Knowledge, it has been proved, is not enough. We have more institutions of higher learning than any nation on the face of the earth. They have been immensely helpful in imparting facts. Our educational institutions have given us skills so that we have been able to produce material goods to the amazement of the world. We have studied the past systematically, we have probed and dissected. This has all been good. But we live our lives with emotions. All the great things that will happen to us —love, marriage, parenthood, joy, humor, inspiration, are on the emotional plane where knowledge and skill of the intellect alone have little bearing. When we look at education as a whole the important question is: *Has there been a corresponding change in attitude?* Have we understood ourselves any better? Are we more at peace with ourselves and others? Does life have more "meaning" for us? Have we a better understanding of our relationship to God? Have we really *learned?* Learning, in the final analysis, means a *change in behavior.*

What We Have Learned

From this point of view it is interesting to examine the progress of some of the individual cases in the student Prayer Therapy class.

Here is one girl who had made up her mind as early as October not to go home for Christmas. Summer vacation gave her enough, if not too much, of her mother's company. "She's so good at everything I can't ever hope to match her," she admitted and when her grades dropped to D's, she tried to sever all home ties. Full of struggle and tension, she perpetually suffered attacks of asthma, anemia, stomach trouble or nervous exhaustion. Her tests indicated "arthritis a possibility unless adequate help ensues."

A girl with a brilliant IQ, a lovely face and a particularly splendid smile, she was suffering through a timid,

abnormal college life to avoid a more abnormal home relationship. The more effort she put forth the more tense
and unfit she became.

Her initial slips forced her to come to terms with her
enmity toward her mother. She learned the futility of
competition on the level of personality. "A microscope
showed me God didn't make two hairs on my head alike,"
she said, "I didn't need to be constantly comparing myself with Mother. God gave her talents and gave me
others. He also gave her a head start."

Next she realized that her inferior feelings were based
on a resentment of her brilliant mind, a sense of obligations and responsibility, of too much to live up to, too
much expected. In prayer she experienced a *change of
feeling*. I know it now for gratitude . . . first to God that
He had entrusted me with a free gift. I knew as long
as I felt inferior, rated myself low, I was actually un-
grateful to Him, and to Mom and Dad and a long line
of wonderful teachers who had poured their free gifts
all round me. But without gratitude I was grudging about
being beholden, about accepting. Honestly, gratitude
freed me of resentment. It's a swell housecleaner."

It also brought an immediate and dramatic reversal in
her life. She went home for Christmas determined to let
the newfound emotion loose. Her mother's efficiency and
reserve melted before it and the following semester, her
tensions released, her health improved and her grades
rose to a B average.

In the case of the junior, football star and fraternity
man, he entered the class because of "interest in the
value of prayer. I thought too that self-understanding
would help me in life."

He and most of the students belonged to that "Easter-
Xmas-sometimes-Sunday-always-in-a-pinch" type of Christianity. "My previous concept of God was intangible.
Sometimes a fellow with a beard up in the clouds. On
good days I had a pleasant feeling toward Him and
thought He might be Spirit. On bad days I wasn't sure
He was at all."

His first reaction to the slips was resentment, skepticism. "Holy cow," he thought. "This fellow generalizes. This could be anyone." Then came something specific. The tester, without any hints, pegged his home problems "like he had read my mail."

His father was an alcoholic and, although he provided a very good living, the atmosphere for the boy and his mother was one of embarrassment and lurking fear. He had lost respect for fatherly authority, but above all he missed his dad.

"Without the slip hitting me in the face, I probably never would have admitted my resentment even to myself. 'Honor thy father' was the right thing to do and I mistakenly thought it would be more comfortable to pretend I did. Only I had to go back to the guy I knew when I was 7, before the drinking started, a wonderful guy who used to take me hunting and fishing. So I honored that father and froze out this stranger who had usurped his place.

"It was the end of the first semester before I learned, through very honest prayer, to put myself in his shoes. 'All right,' I said. 'My Dad's got a problem. Maybe I could help!' "

He decided the resentment might not be one-sided. Had he been the very best son? Maybe too his dad was suffering, not celebrating, trying to escape a few of the demons the boy had met in himself, fear, guilt, the unholy four.

The first week-end he could he went home, determined to make his father understand that "drunk or sober, he was my Dad and I accepted him." The proffered friendship was clutched with pathetic eagerness by the older man. Barriers melted so fast the son found himself explaining Prayer Therapy to his father. For the first time the drink problem was squarely faced, God's help asked.

"The outward things improve in a sort of equal proportion to the improvement in my prayer life," the boy said. "It's wonderful, instead of falling into bed muttering now-I-lay-me-down-to-sleep-take-care-of-me-God . . . if you're around . . . to be praying intelligently to something I understand guided by feelings."

A nineteen-year-old lad expressed it thus: *"Prayer finally comes to mean not to express an opinion, but to feel a Presence."*

Next to an improved concept of God and increased prayer power, the most important change these young Prayer Therapy students claimed was "a new set of values."

Said one senior, "I had it all computed on the material sliderule by financial success. I couldn't miss. Already I had friends, popularity, top grades. I was a wheel. Now, turn this ability to making money and I'd go right to the top. Swimming pools, cars, wall-to-wall carpeting. Eureka! Happiness! What business? Any business so long as there was dough in it."

Following a year of Prayer Therapy he had decided to become a clinical psychologist making use of our new techniques. "I am still positive I'll succeed," he said. "I just have a different idea of success. The most important thing is not going out and making dollars. It's going inside and making peace. This way I'll realize exactly what Love wishes to give so I know I won't have to worry about getting it or keeping it. I'm no great shakes as a Bible student but I've been rereading it and I think this is what Jesus meant by 'seeking first the kingdom of God . . . within you . . .' and the rest being added."

This was no isolated instance. Another senior frankly admitted he wanted power. To him, knowledge was the path to riches, riches to power. He watched others graduate heavy with knowledge and fail to grab the plums. With him it would be different and he entered the Prayer class to find out if prayer really had a creative power, any kind of power.

It was he who said: "I knew it would lull and quiet women, but would it accomplish anything concrete? I want to observe the laboratory effect on the others . . . the guinea pigs."

After a few weeks of observation he began to speculate on what it might do to *him*. He accepted the challenge, took his desire for power into prayer and came out with the same motive redirected. He found the real power was not in his bank account or his knowledge, but in himself, in his inner contact with the invisible principle that declared itself visibly in the heavens and earth.

"There's a lot of so-called power loose in the world, much of it financial, none of it permanent," he decided. "For that you have to be interested in getting, not giving. There's no circulation. It isn't elegant to say but it's obvious that this creates a block, a mental and spiritual constipation. I suffered from it when I started studying Prayer Therapy.

"Real power I came to understand as something you give out with, not what you have or take in materially. Whatever you're giving out with is proof of how much inner power you've contacted and how clear you've kept the release lines."

As he re-formed his ideas of power this 21-year-old began to be very selective in his direction of it. "A dynamo will light a city or supply the spark for an explosion," he figured. "Since Love is the basis of Power it can't be used against the universe but you can choose to make yourself pretty uncomfortable. In Biblical language they said, 'As ye sow, so shall ye reap.' To find this power coupled with free choice gives enormous hope and meaning to every individual life."

Even the campus "wolf" had a change of values. Money in reverse was the root of his evils, for he was to inherit a very large sum. His tests pointed to a "person living in a day-dream world . . . tremendous desire to please . . . starved for assurance he is accepted as self."

In self-honesty he admitted he wanted to be sure he wasn't being loved for his money, that his financial position had no bearing on his popularity. Thoroughly mixed up he felt the only sure proof would be to receive affection solely as a man . . . hence the whistles and wolf-calls.

In Prayer Therapy sex problems were treated exactly as any others. Sex, they came to understand, was so basic, so strong that unhappy people put undue emphasis on it. Abnormal sex they found another misdirected energy, another form of misguided love, and as with hate, it could destroy the individual.

"I know now I turned to it as an attempt to bolster my ego, to feel needed, wanted, secure . . . in other words, loved. Actually, using the four steps on it I came to understand it was simply the highest form of love I had reached."

Not pleased to regard his prowess as a simple case of immaturity, of stunted emotional response, he felt if he couldn't grow to a higher understanding of love, develop a more lasting and trustworthy measure of security, his path could lead from that of a frisky young wolf to a balding oldster who was all whistle.

Regularly and positively he tried to see himself as loving and loved by God and others in every act of his life, rich or poor. As his prayer life increased his insecurity decreased and the whistles subsided to a normal chirp and finally to his engagement to a pretty fellow-student.

"It will have a lasting effect on my marriage," he thinks, "to recognize sex as an outgrowth of love, a complementary part, and not expect it to come the other way round. It is risky to trust sex to grow into love but it took Prayer Therapy to show me the difference."

The student atheist and agnostic provided interesting responses. The agnostic, high on "exact science," said in effect, "God is unknowable. He may or may not exist. You can't prove it and I don't know him."

He attended out of curiosity and, particularly embarrassed by the quick freedom and enthusiasm with which the others discussed their experiences in prayer, he found it rough going at first. Eventually that very thing made the first dent in his armor.

"The instruction to Christians to 'let their light so shine before men that they may see your good works and glorify your father' was given by a master psychologist," he said. "I think 'they' are guys like me."

He found himself envying the others their experiences, their increased joy. He felt shut out. He had to admit, at the very bottom of his being, a deep sense of futility, and the age old question, "Does life have a meaning?" His fellows seemed to have found one. He had not.

Half-fearfully, he took his sense of futility into prayer. Could he simply start with the will to faith, without the genuine article? It seemed he could. "I began to expect and get results. Feelings. Joys. The certainty. Through personal experience I could know a Supreme Being."

The atheist came to humor a friend. She "knew there was no God," when she entered the class and left still "knowing there is no God" but with a difference.

She had been robbed of her faith in a heavenly Father by the behavior of His children. A tomboy, and very homely, she was badgered and teased without mercy in grammar school. Bitter, with a tremendous anxiety, a psychologist failed to help her in her junior year in high. She became a fatalist, a pessimist, unwilling to make any effort or contribution toward life. "I could be snuffed out in that car tomorrow," she said. "Why bother today?"

She, too, saw evidence in the class of a power for good, especially in the case of her friend, but she clung to her closed mind and threw her intellect into rationalizing the results. When she raised taunting objections young Jim Parker wisely let the class answer them.

She was a psychology major and simple logic couldn't answer her involved intellectual quirks and for some months she continued to jeer politely. Eventually the very thing that drove her from her childhood God brought her the first adult glimpse of Him, the behavior of His children. She suffered a serious loss and no amount of intellectualism could meet her grief. The only thing she had to hang onto was the emotion of love expressed as caring, the actual brotherly love mediated to her by the Prayer Therapy class.

"Love is certainly a power," she admitted afterward. "I still don't believe in God but I do believe in the power of Love." Nor did the charitable class point out that, call it what she liked, infinite Love was exactly what they had found God to be.

Here we are back at Jung's statement that "Whether you call the principle of existence 'God,' 'matter,' 'energy,' or anything else you like, you have created nothing; you have simply changed a symbol." The important point is that, whether atheist, agnostic, or true believer, every single student who honestly attempted Prayer Therapy *learned* something—there was a corresponding *change in attitude, a change in behavior*.

If we wish to measure our progress from day to day, regardless of our age or situation, it will not matter one bit how many written examinations we could pass on the subject of Prayer Therapy, how many Biblical quotations we have memorized, how many high ideals we have borrowed from another. This is all on the intellectual level. We have not *learned* a thing unless we can see and feel an emotional change, a new attitude, and a subsequent change in behavior. Then, and only then, will our world become new.

11

HOW TO APPROACH
SELF-HONESTY

WE RETURN NOW TO THE KEY WHICH PRAYER THERAPY students used to release their burdens, frustrations, miseries, and start them on their road to freedom. It was to *make prayer a practice in honesty*.

It is important to stress once again that daring to be honest with ourselves *about* ourselves is only the preliminary to direct prayer. Direct prayer, as our point of contact with a God of Love, is the healing power. But, as we saw in earlier chapters on the Kingdom within and the Four Demons, an honest evaluation is necessary to recognize our present drives and attitudes, reactions and responses. Then, and then only, do we have a basis for change, a direction for specific prayer.

The Random Prayers prayed fervently without this step and failed. Klaus, the orange rancher, the society woman, all the Prayer Therapy students sought first to discover what they really were today, what they did not wish to be, and were then in a position to become what God surely intended them to be—whole of mind and body.

Prelude to Prayer

Psychology has provided us with excellent methods for getting to know ourselves. It has proven conclusively that most of us hide from our conscious knowing the very things causing our discomforts and then offered us new understanding, new ways for honest self-evaluation that go beyond the obvious sins of omission and commission. To do us any good this fresh knowledge must be *used*. It is not a theory but a tool. We must apply it to ourselves. What we need is to understand precisely how to do that.

This chapter and the following one are designed to introduce you to your present "self." They are guides to help you take inventory of your actual emotional content. If honestly followed they can give you the insight necessary to begin to change your world today. When you have finished them you should know definitely what your past direction has been, whether toward a more abundant life, or toward being inactive, worn out.

Once you consciously know these things, the choice is yours.

A few words of warning before you begin. Under no circumstances should any of your discoveries about yourself lead to self-condemnation. Quite the reverse. It is a point for self-congratulation if we are ready and mature enough to face what we honestly are and what we have to work with. Remember that we are what we are today because of many things: education, conditioning, environment, tradition, culture, and in many cases, our own or another's ignorance. Some of the things we may find surprising or disconcerting in our personality make-up were shaped long before we had a reasoned, conscious choice in the matter. Right here we will determine that all blame shall cease whether directed toward ourselves or another.

If, however, we do not like what we find, and yet make no effort to change, then we can blame no one else if tomorrow finds us no better off than today. Our discoveries confirmed that an honest effort resulted in honest improvement. Thus we alone hold dominion and direct our destiny.

Again, this is not a short course in psychoanalysis or depth analysis. All the indications you are asked to recognize here are within reach of your conscious mind. Consciousness can be likened to a City in darkness where the Lord Mayor (I, my conscious, choosing self) directs a searchlight capable of illuminating one section after another. That is precisely what we do daily. From ten to eleven we may require the focus of the mind in the area of mathematics, from eleven to twelve the creative faculty, a desirable day dream, our knowledge of cookery and so forth. But a great deal of the City we never call upon, although it is always there. The slums, for instance, we prefer to remain forever outside the reach of our searchlight, although the malodor and contamination spreads contagion throughout other areas. Now we are prepared to be bold, to illuminate these unvisited, unwanted places. We begin our slum clearance by a tour of the City so that we shall know exactly where the workmanship of prayer is needed to eliminate and rebuild.

You can see that each of us can make this tour within *our own* consciousness. Here alone are we Lord Mayor. We will be just as unable to take the other fellow's inventory as we were in the beginning. It does not lie within our capabilities even if it lay within our province, which it decidedly does not.

Yet one more warning. This is not Operation Bootstrap. Our City will not be rebuilt in a night as obviously as it did not achieve its present design in a day. Even Saul of Tarsus, bloodthirsty persecutor of the Christians, who experienced the soul shaking vision of Christ on the road to Damascus, had to spend long days consolidating and proving his new way of life before he became the Apostle Paul, greatest of the Christian missionaries. Give yourself and the power of prayer time to work until the leaven can permeate every recess of consciousness with its healing power. All any of us need require of ourselves is that we show measurable progress in the right direction—in this case growth along sounder, happier, healthier lines.

No scoring system has been recommended, for to label your findings "Excellent—good—fair—poor" implies comparison of one individual against another. This is not pertinent. It is only important to measure yourself today against the self you would like to be and then check your progress after a month of applied Prayer Therapy. In another five months, if you have brought sincerity and perseverance to your experiment, a review of these chapters should show you that the real comparison lies between you as you are now, in some degree of suffering and bondage, and the Self being reborn, the free man created in God's image, knowing the fullness of peace, wholeness, usefulness.

The points to be kept in mind as you set about your evaluation are first, that this is simply the prelude to direct prayer and will be used in conjunction with the specific techniques recommended in the next chapter; second, that it will prove a guide to self-knowledge only if you bring to it a true desire and intent to be honest with yourself; third, that it will serve the future purpose of a yardstick for measuring your progress or backsliding.

It is suggested that you take pencil and paper and keep your evaluations for later comparison. Do not, however, review the chapter more than once a month. You are measuring growth. Then allow for measurable improvement secure in the knowledge that from your first effort, however feeble, you are moving in the right direction. Above all, regardless of what reveals itself to you, there will be no self-condemnation. On the contrary remember that a vital step toward freeing yourself has been accomplished with the initial will toward honesty. What is required is to know the truth about self, as you are today, see the truth of this Self as God intended it to be. When this gap has been bridged by prayer then you will be free indeed.

Recognizing Our Defense Mechanisms

On almost any souvenir stand you can find a statue of three little monkeys who are supposed to represent a very moral philosophy. One covers his eyes, one his ears and one his mouth. They represent See-no-evil, Hear-no-evil, and Speak-no-evil. Now this might be very commendable indeed if we applied it in our conduct toward others. Unfortunately, the chief application we make is in relationship to ourselves. Such an attitude keeps us from any painful view into the actual state in our inner Kingdom.

Psychology calls any variation on this attitude a defense mechanism. By defense mechanism is meant that to keep from looking at our real feelings or admitting our anxiety feelings, we literally escape from them by building up a defense mechanism or wall protecting our ego from any disagreeable knowledge of itself. We actually become self-deluded and it is impossible for us to be honest with ourselves. We find ourselves then in the exact state of the three monkeys, blind, deaf, and mute, and this is a frustrating state indeed.

The fact is that a troublesome feeling or emotion must be seen to be destroyed. Thus the first step in self-honesty is to recognize our defense mechanisms and get behind the wall. Here are listed four common defense mechanisms. If you will honestly answer the questions following each you will have a strong indication as to whether you have been hiding from yourself—and the method you may have used.

Denial is the first line of defense. You will remember that the child, when fear or guilt first strikes at his ego, may begin asking, "I didn't break that, did I, Mother?" We are, at this point, actually aware that we *have* broken something, but by affirming the lie and trying to believe differently, we feel safer, more comfortable. If we can get Mother, or anyone else, to confirm our denial, we feel better still. Far from outgrowing this tendency, unless we face it and resolve it somewhere along the line, it outgrows our conscious control and we can lie successfully to ourselves and others about things causing guilt or unpleasantness.

It is important to recognize that prayer itself can be denial. Positive or affirmative prayer is successful *only* when preceded by self-honesty. We cannot look at the shattered bits in our lives, whether a broken dish, a broken home, or a painful body, and positively affirm that this is not the case without self-deception. Only as we look to the cause, disobedience, carelessness, malice, hatred, fear or whatever, and recognize it, surrender it, and *then* affirm that inharmony of any name or nature is not in line with the Law of Love do we change the present situation or improve one iota the chance of such a pattern repeating itself in our lives.

If you suspect that this defense has been allowed to deceive you ask yourself:

1. Do I habitually or even sometimes feel like saying something way down deep and refuse to voice it or express it even to myself? (This is a soul searching question and you can well afford to give it some time. Include your relations toward the people with whom you are most often in contact, whether family or businesswise. Watch for resentment even toward people you actually should be fond of, your attitude toward your work, your home, toward God and prayer.)

2. Do I often preface my remarks with, "Well, one thing about *me* is, *I* never" talk about my neighbors, or kick a man when he's down, etc. (This is a common symptom of denial—to recognize in others what we feel in ourselves and immediately deny that such a trait could belong to us.)

3. Do I know the truth and live and speak a lie? (Remember that, even when truth would appear painful and the lie wears a pleasant face, you are changing nothing by simply glossing it over.)

4. Do I go to God in prayer refusing to face any need for change and simply insisting that everything is lovely, myself included? (If so, you cling to or bury what is amiss, and God Himself can do nothing against your will. If you have experimented before with positive prayer only to be disappointed by results, look into this question carefully. Recognition and surrender *must* preface your positive prayer.)

Rationalization. This is another of our frequent methods of self-deceit. Mr. Smith has been fired from his job. He says, "Well, I don't mind. It wasn't a very good job anyway and I had a stupid boss." He needs to rationalize to protect his good opinion of himself. It would be too painful to say, "I wasn't doing my job very well, I was so resentful against authority that I kept making mistakes and actually wasn't worth what they were paying me." Or perhaps we don't get asked to the most exciting social event of the year or miss the boat on a promotion or election to some club office we badly wanted. Disappointment is understandable. It could spur us to a new and more successful effort. But we are defeated if we rationalize our true feelings by saying, "I don't care. There are lots of things I'd rather do. It's a lousy outfit anyhow." This attitude may seem noble or brave but it is not. Why? Because it is a lie, and simply buries our resentment. It is only through the truth that we can take action and become free.

In correcting this tendency it is not necessary at first that we admit the truth of our real feelings to anyone but God and ourselves. The time will come, as we practice truth, when we are able quite painlessly to do so, however, and the release will be tremendous. When we rationalize, those who love us tend to compound our falseness to spare our feelings although most often they are already aware how the situation truly stands. Forcing them to agree with our deceit we lose the opportunity for their genuine help and understanding and may eventually sacrifice their respect.

Misguided prayer can itself be used to rationalize in a most subtle way. Remember, our defense mechanisms help us to hide any need for or effort to "repent" or "change our minds." What finer evasion can we use than to say it is God's will that we suffer greatly in this world and are not required to mend any but the obvious sins until Hereafter when the change will be made for us, wings and all, if we have been "good"?

To recognize whether rationalization has cheated you of insight, question your responses during a given day.

1.   Do I try to think of a reason for anything disagreeable that occurs which makes me look good to myself and others?

2.   Do I, instead of acting to change a situation, use my mental abilities and energies to explain it away?

3.   Do I feel that, if I had been given the opportunity, I could be more successful than my boss, the president of my club, or any person in authority over me?

4.   When I pray do I explain to myself, either directly or indirectly, that Fate or Providence or God or Luck has set my difficulties upon me and I must therefore accept them now and hope for a better break later?

Projection. This is far more subtle and damaging than the two defense mechanisms we have observed. We use this device when certain unacceptable thoughts, wishes or impulses try to penetrate consciousness. The method is to refute them for ourselves by attributing them to others. Too often the undesirable qualities we see in those around us are merely those weaknesses submerged in ourselves.

Here is a student who keeps insisting her professor doesn't like her. She is so afraid to express her resentment even to herself that she cannot admit she doesn't like the professor and turns it around to project that thought onto him. Unless she can learn to be honest about her feelings very little if anything can be done to improve the relationship. Why? Because nothing can or needs to be done about the professor's "negative" feelings. He has none. He is an unconscious target. Nothing more. The student requires insight in this area to show her that the only way for the professor to "like her" is for her to clear up her own feelings in the matter and find the error has disappeared.

Here is a wife who constantly criticizes her husband for being inconsiderate or a husband who finds fault because his wife is domineering. Each most probably possesses the weakness they project into the other but feel these to be unworthy in themselves and so find self-honesty too difficult. It is the person disturbed within himself that gives the most time to fault-finding in others, quite literally a dirty pot calling a clean kettle black.

Projection can be determined and identified in our personality make-up by an honest examination on these points:

1. Do I feel that people in authority don't like me very well?

2. Do I feel that unkindness and lack of love is the general condition in the world, my country, community, home, that I see it all about me? (If you can answer "yes" to this you should question very earnestly this absence of kindness and love in your own true feelings.)

3. Can I honestly examine myself and say that the things for which I most often criticize others are not strongly present within me?

Reaction-Formation. This mechanism is perhaps the most subtle of all our illusions about ourselves. It means, quite simply, that we have perfected the technique of doing and pretending the exact opposite of what we feel so well that we believe them ourselves. When the cause is violent and the reaction formation has been equally violent it erupts on the front pages of our newspapers as the dear, sweet old gentleman who wouldn't harm a fly but quite suddenly beats his 40-year-old wife to death with a poker. This has the earmarks to the uninitiated of sudden insanity. Actually it is more likely to be the slow intensity of resentment and hatred carefully masked behind this defense mechanism until the personality control crumbles beneath the pressure.

While this is an extreme example the symptoms of this defense are generally a cloying sweetness, a tendency to gush and carry on in a favorable manner about the particular thing or person where violent contrary emotions are present.

The impotent man will talk constantly of sex. The wife who actually deeply resents her husband will talk interminably about his good points and her devotion. A mother whose children are obviously out of control and a source of deep shame and resentment to her will dwell out of all proportion on how "cute" they are when they break her hostess's best China.

In this degree it sounds frivolous and laughable but it is never so. This violent reaction *away* from our true feelings indicates an equally violent and painful buried emotion in that precise area, often our deepest hatreds and resentments. The physical symptoms which manifest from the glossed-over dynamite under the reaction-formation are numerous and yet it will be the hardest for us to admit to ourselves. It is particularly painful because those who have hidden behind it are very apt to believe they *are* the thoroughly sweet and loving being they have pretended to be.

Recognizing the danger of this defense will help us to make an all-out effort to uncover it in our inner world. Ask yourself:

1. Have I told myself lies about people (or a person) until I now believe those lies and have lost touch with the actual person and my honest response to them?

2. Am I constantly covering up hostility through fear that the other person might know and my desire to completely fool them?

3. Do I think of myself as a sweet, kindly person, yet have a frequent sensation of "holding myself in" to support that concept?

4. Can I sit alone and think honestly about my feelings for individuals? (This seems easy but you might try it. If you can make a beginning here, particularly if you have answered "yes" to the above questions, you are already breaking the hypnosis of the reaction-formation.)

Once we have identified our defense mechanisms we can no longer be completely deceived by them. We will see them for what they are, foe, not friend, and day by day as the temptation comes to deny or rationalize, project or invert our true feelings we can begin on the spot to reverse that impulse and to look honestly at what we find.

Telltale Signs

After recognizing our defenses we can look a little further and see whether we are displaying any outward signs which indicate something amiss in our internal economy.

First we ask some of the obvious questions which indicate what kind of person we are at the surface level. Do we get along well with our friends or are we quarrelsome, touchy? Do we work well with others and how often do they annoy us? Are we often down-hearted? Or elated? Are we overly dramatic where everything is described as "marvelous," "perfect," "divine," "appalling"?

Are we indecisive to such a degree that we qualify everything we say? Are we tense most of the time? Do we take refuge in a nervous habit, sniff, continually clear our throats, and so on? Are we so fluent that we rattle on and on interspersing our conversation with strained laughter? Do we find it hard to make our thoughts clear to others? Are we continually tired? Do we feel that life is pointless, not worth while?

This can be individually elaborated, for it is easy enough, if we are in earnest and willing to stop a moment and think, to "see ourselves as others see us." Since none of us are perfect we will all find things on this level which we wish changed or improved.

Going a step farther we begin to catalogue feelings and moods which only we ourselves truly can know anything about and which indicate a greater degree of discord in the Kingdom within. If our search reveals us to be the silent, inhibited type we might as well face at the outset that we have been a great burden to ourselves, turning everything inward, and that our journey will be more difficult than that of the overly aggressive person. If we have been overly aggressive we can be pretty certain that we have been more troublesome to others and that our human relations have suffered. Let us look carefully, then, for these telltale signs:

Depression. By depression we mean that one is dejected, or low in spirits, or just feeling blue. We invariably feel hopeless and inadequate. Twenty per cent more women than men suffer from depression.

What are some of the reasons for this state of mind? One is a lack of feeling of relatedness to others, to God and the Universe. Or a feeling of uselessness, of having no place in the scheme of things. High on the list is a feeling of having committed or thought of having committed "the unpardonable sin." The "sin" is of an indefinite nature. Since "sin" to the depressed person means death, thoughts of suicide are not uncommon.

Since there is no unpardonable sin, anyone suffering from depression must see that this childish attitude may be a desire to return to a more infantile state where one is given protective care. This desire is a retreat from reality.

Withdrawal. Retreating from others and from life is a common symptom of a faulty emotional adjustment. We "suffer in silence." The burden of imagined guilt may be so strong that we feel deep inside ourselves that we ought to suffer, but to keep from getting hurt we withdraw to ourselves alone. Those who withdraw deeply need the love and companionship of others, but are afraid of it and consequently do not know how to respond if it is offered them. Self-blame is so great and hostility often so strong that the sufferer is terrified to an extent where he cannot or will not face life.

Delusions. A delusion is usually in direct conflict with truth and fact. It is a false belief. Obviously, as with all these telltale symptoms they can be present in us to a greater or lesser degree. All of us at times pretend to be something we are not. But these pretenses can get out of hand. Then we do not know who or what we are.

The most common are delusions of grandeur and delusions of persecution. Again there are degrees. Sometimes those with delusions of grandeur carry their wishes or desires to absurd extremes. They may believe they are Napoleon, Eisenhower, or even God. Others believe they have tremendous personal power and by thought waves are influencing numerous people. Some religious fanatics not only come dangerously close but actually would fall into this category.

Delusions of persecution may start with the attitude that "everyone is against me," and progress to the idea that "someone is trying to get rid of me by poisoning my coffee." Again, religious groups that believe the "hell-fire and brimstone" philosophy more often than not suffer delusions of persecution.

Compulsions. Most of us in some way follow a set pattern in our daily living. This is good. Order is a basic necessity to accomplishment. However, when the occasion arises we are flexible enough to change. Some people are so compulsive that they carry out their daily tasks as a ritual. These must always be the same without any deviation. Should something interrupt this pattern they are miserable and unable to cope successfully. Others feel compelled to wash their hands continually, or to "take things" which more often than not they do not need.

Hypochondria. This is described as a morbid depression of mind or spirits, specifically in the medical profession a morbid anxiety about one's own health which conjures up imaginary ailments.

An appalling number of people fasten imaginary illnesses or disorders (not to be confused with psychosomatic illnesses where symptoms are real enough but not organically caused) in an unconscious attempt to get attention (love) or to escape responsibility. To rid oneself of this means, first, to admit the tendency and then face the fact that it does not accomplish the desired result. Compulsory attention is not love but the payment of blackmail and responsibilities shunted off on another rob us of our primary life functions, accomplishment and fulfillment.

Take a woman who married an exceptionally attractive man but was so filled with self-doubt in her ability to "hold" him through love that she took to her bed and "held" him through imaginary illnesses until she died of her first genuine ailment 20 years later. But did she "hold" him in any real sense of the word? Once she abandoned her responsibilities as a wife there was no normal companionship, and both lived in great misery and real bondage to her inability to face life or trust the power of Love.

Granted this is an extreme case, but if we find ourselves "enjoying" ill health we must look to see whether we secretly believe it has rewards of either a spiritual or material nature. To believe there is spiritual gain in magnifying suffering is to insult the Deity. There can be no merit in shunting off the purpose for which we were sent into the world. And any gain in human attention so derived is only a counterfeit of the real thing.

Psychosomatic Symptoms. Here, we remember, we deal with genuine bodily ailments where the physical disorder or discomfort is induced by emotional rather than organic factors. These symptoms indicate that we have buried our emotional conflicts and, in order to cope with these buried feelings, we develop a symptom. We must recall that the symptom is not as dangerous or damaging to the personality as the suppression of the emotional disorder. For anyone who finds himself in bondage to psychosomatic illness the first step is to recognize that *fear* is the motivating power behind our suppressions.

Since alcoholism is an illness rooted in emotional disturbance we must try to see what lies below the surface and drives the unhappy individual to try and escape through drink. In a study done with the Rorschach Test the following findings were revealed:

He (the alcoholic) is a maladjusted, immature individual who has developed few techniques for alleviating his feelings of discomfort. Actually his attitude implies that he will not recognize limitations or inadequacies in his personality, will not admit them. In order to convince himself that he has no need to compromise or inhibit his reactions, he deliberately exposes himself to irritating and challenging stimuli instead of insulating himself against them. There is a certain "grandiosity," a certain omnipotence in such behavior. This refusal to accept his personality problems in a way that would enable him to work with them and build up the more acceptable forms of compensation is one of the most striking characteristics of the alcoholic personality as revealed in the Rorschach Test protocols. If he cannot accept the idea of limitation and inadequacy, the conflict must be outside himself, and he proceeds to externalize it.*

We can see that the alcoholic, like the rest of us, needs quite thoroughly to accept the fact that the Kingdom of Heaven—or Hell—is within him. Then he will be in a position to begin ridding himself of the emotions causing his discomfort.

Alcoholics Anonymous, which has done such a splendid job in helping the "drunk," has insisted that the ability to be honest with himself is an absolute necessity to the individual's recovery. From there, following twelve inspiring steps, they seek with God's help to eliminate the "defects of character," which their self-honesty has uncovered. The results for those who have earnestly followed their program has been a sober return to society and happy, useful lives.

The psychosomatic disorders prevalent today would fill many texts if they were all treated thoroughly. We need to look at the more common ones. They are (1) Peptic Ulcer, (2) Asthma, (3) Migraine Headache, (4) Rheumatoid Arthritis, (5) Functional Heart Trouble, (6) Acne.

(1) *Peptic Ulcer.* An open sore in the duodenum commonly characterizes the peptic ulcer. It will invariably be related to the emotional state of the individual. While some may only have "nervous indigestion," if the emotional stress is of sufficient severity or over a prolonged period of time, the individual will probably develop an ulcer. People with ulcers commonly voice the flattering opinion that it is due to overwork. It would be more

* *Studies of Compulsive Drinkers,* by H. Wortis, L. R. Sillman, and F. Halpern, Hillhouse Press, 1946.

accurately stated that, because of the nervous tensions and emotional conditions, he cannot accomplish with ease and pleasure but drives himself in a kind of frenzy. He may have an over-developed need for success and money (both symbols of love to him), or he may unconsciously feel the need to suffer hardships to atone for buried guilt. Ulcers are caused by "lack of love," or misguided love, and an inability to express resentments without feeling guilty.

(2) *Asthma*. Asthma is bronchial neurosis. The asthmatic would like to do his own breathing but doesn't feel secure enough to do it all on his own. Often there is hostility toward his parents, but a fear of being separated from them, hence the child will cling to the parents. Because of the wheezing, the parents in turn develop an overly protective attitude which usually makes the condition worse. A child may attempt to control the actions of parents by asthmatic attacks.

(3) *Rheumatoid Arthritis*. This is characteristic of the very hostile. The sufferer literally seethes with hostility. This is held within, consequently not understood, and comes forth in the form of arthritis.

(4) *Migraine*. Migraine headache involves at least five per cent of the population with two-thirds of all sufferers women. It may grow in intensity so that vomiting occurs. Generally it locates on one side of the head. Careful studies of migraine patients show them to be perfectionists, intolerant, unduly upset by stress, having a terrific drive for success, and difficulty in sexual adjustment. Women who have migraine should look to see whether the label "domineering" fits.

(5) *Functional Heart Trouble*. Heart trouble is a growing concern. One out of every two people over fifty years of age has heart trouble. How much of this may be due to tension is speculative, but it is appallingly high.

(6) *Acne*. Acne is a way of punishing self; punishing self to the degree that the opposite sex will not be attracted to the individual. They want to attract the op-

posite sex but are afraid of their own feelings, so punish themselves rather than face these feelings.

In discussing the peptic ulcer another telltale sign of emotional disorder was mentioned—an over-developed interest in money. *Avarice* or greed we have been taught to regard as "sin." It would be more healthful for us to accept it for what it is, an almost unfailing indication that we somehow feel cut off from love, and try to fill this void by making money a substitute. It will not work. There *is* no substitute for love. So, if we find that an abnormal desire for money beyond our just wants and pleasures possesses us, it would be well to have an honest look at what lies behind this drive. The same could be said of excessive *envy, jealousy,* and the other so-called "sins" of character which we can easily identify if they are present within us. These are always signals that somewhere the Law of Love is not functioning harmoniously. The *Will to Fail* we have discussed quite fully in a preceding chapter, but we must call it to mind again and question ourselves to see if it is manifesting in our individual life.

It is impossible to conclude our list of telltale signs without bringing *self-righteousness* into focus. If we find ourselves feeling self-righteous it is an authentic indication that all is not well within. We encountered it in the mother-in-law who suffered so greatly from hate. We saw it impeding the early progress of the ineffectual minister. And it can impede our own progress immeasurably. It supports all the strong defense mechanisms which keep us from knowing ourselves. It simply and finally precludes any suspicion on our part that we are not already perfect.

Goodness and beauty, purity and truth have no need to toot their own horns. Self-righteousness, on the other hand, is most verbal. It is a state of consciousness wherein we constantly compare ourselves to others and always come out on top. The need to do this lies as surely in the presence of a buried demon, fear, guilt, hate, inferiority feelings, as do alcoholism or depression.

The danger in self-righteousness is that at first it does

not seem to give us pain. And it is not easy for us to de-
tect in ourselves. Sooner or later it will do great harm to
our human relationships and its cousins, which are many
and varied, will come to live with it. We will find ill-
temper (the vice of the virtuous) under the same roof.
Criticism, domineeringness, self-satisfaction (as sure a
way to stunt further progress as has yet been uncovered),
self-justification (rationalization in full flower) all thrive
in the ground of self-righteousness.

Because this symptom usually manifests in people who
"keep the law" to a large degree and regard themselves
as very *good* individuals, it is actually necessary to look
further before they will accept it as a danger signal. We
need not go beyond the conclusion of that masterly
story, The Prodigal Son. The prodigal, we know, came
home. But many of us forget what happened to his
brother. This other son who had never gone away, who
had lived an exemplary life probably abiding by the Ten
Commandments, saw his wayward brother return, receive the ring, the robe, the Father's kiss. And his resentment was so great that he sulked and would not go in.

So humility brought the prodigal, the sinner, who had
known pain and sorrow and suffering, back to the Father's
house—and self-righteousness drove the "good" son out
at the last moment.

It is never enough to live by the law. The law without
love is void, dead, availeth nothing. If you find self-
righteousness present in your consciousness set to work
at once to perfect your sense of love, to find your error
and cast it out, before you are cast out of the Kingdom
of Harmony where you *know* you belong.

12

TECHNIQUES FOR
SELF-KNOWLEDGE

AT THIS POINT WE ARE AWARE OF OUR DEFENSE mechanisms and have looked for any telltale signs manifesting in our make-up. Before we directly attack the techniques for identifying our particular demons we should know that there is more than one area in which we may find flaws. Our tendency is to believe that "myself" is always my total being. But there are several selves; the social self, the intellectual self, the emotional self, and, in Prayer Therapy, we are always careful to remember that these "selves" of human conditioning are but distortions of the spiritual Self, created in God's image, free and perfect.

The value of recognizing these different areas is that we can avoid the trap of finding a weakness in one and then condemning "myself" in toto. The thoroughly negative "confession" which blankets the prayer with the burden of being "a miserable sinner, a worm," is not only unsuccessful, it is a lie. We must evaluate our strengths along with our weaknesses if we are to have a really thorough knowledge of ourselves and avoid the self-condemnation that defeats us before we begin.

If our difficulty lies in the sexual area only we must refuse to weaken our strong points by forcing them to carry the burden under blanket condemnation of the "whole man." Suppose we find that excessive criticism and resentment are marring our response to our world.

Then what is wanted is some reconstruction in the emotional and social areas but we do not attempt to burn down the intellectual self nor belittle the spiritual self.

There is an old joke that the condemned man was kind to his aged mother. Yet it is possible that he truly was, and that we might have spared him and society much pain had someone, at an earlier stage, isolated his social weakness for rebuilding, while affirming and encouraging this evidence of love in the emotional area.

The psychopath in the asylum may be positively loaded with information. A Phi Beta Kappa key may even prove that his intellectual self has blossomed splendidly. But his capacity to feel what is right (the emotional area) can be practically nil. Possibly the emphasis in his life had been upon instruction when it should have been upon *relationship*. There was not a proper balance between the intellectual and emotional growth.

This is of the utmost importance for we must consciously *choose* to become balanced men and women. Education of the masses is an almost new experiment in the scope of man's evolution and it has made us one-sided in our consideration of the "whole" man. The Four Demons which plague us are *all* in the emotional area, and so we should be in no way surprised if our inventory reveals that most of our difficulties, and those of our children, lie in this currently neglected phase of our total self.

What We Are Evaluating

Here is the way we should question exactly what we are evaluating. Remembering that the total self is the spiritual man, God trying to express through all our facets and talents, we try to find just where we are blocking or distorting that expression.

If you are in doubt as to means for identifying the precise area you can ask: Does this deal primarily with my feelings about myself, my reactions and relations to others? (Emotional Self.) Does this deal primarily with my lack of knowledge or information? (Intellectual Self.) Does this deal primarily with my relationships to my

environment, community, the world in which I live?
(Social Self.)

Wisdom is the fruit of the balanced intellect. Love
(including a proper estimate of ourselves as God's offspring) is the powering of good emotional growth. Harmony (peace, purpose, usefulness) is the proper relationship of the socially mature individual to the world
in which he lives. That is the aim of the balanced personality. The unbalanced personality is *not* bad. It is
simply undeveloped or distorted and the proper aim is
to set this straight.

Looking in All Directions

When we begin our actual fact finding journey into
the kingdom within, we find we have a compass which
directs our attention to four points. We can look Backward—Inward—Outward—Onward.

When we look backward, we question how we came
to be here, and why. This is no leisurely trip down
Memory Lane taking old sentiments off the shelf. That
journey has its proper place. We travel now with alert
mind and specific intent. We recall first our race inheri-
tance, the inspiring and masterful way that man has
traveled down the sweep of ages. The race as a whole
has come a long, long way. We have many inherited
tendencies. A forward motion, a searching and climbing,
an ability to unfold toward greater and seemingly end-
less development. We agree with Emerson that "He
that is once admitted to the right of reason is made a
freeman of the whole estate. What Plato has thought,
he may think, what a saint has felt, he may feel, what
at any time has befallen any man, he can understand."

As for ourselves, we can see enormous growth along
certain lines. Others where we have fallen by the way-
side. We see purity lost. Vision defeated. The point is
that heights once attained can be attained again and so we
regard ourselves at our highest moments as well as the
areas where today we are backsliders.

When we look backward we recognize, without blame
or condemnation, only for the purposes of truth, the ef-

fect of education, association, environment, culture and personal influence. If there are chains, we seek to break them. If there are lacks, we must begin to fill them. If fine things have drifted away many of them are not past recall. No one can take this trip for you. Once it is indicated, you must travel it honestly and alone. Then you will better understand your present position.

To look *Inward* is not only to recognize our strengths, but to face our demons squarely and call them by name. We go beyond the superficial and delve into that personal unconscious where we have stored unwanted material all through the years. We need no further introduction to the Four Demons, Fear, Guilt, Inferiority Feelings, Hate, that are apt to lurk there, but we do need specific techniques for recognizing them. We need to ask ourselves these searching questions on each specific one. Let us take *fear* first:

1. When faced with a specific task, do I feel that I am too small, weak, inferior, and either not try at all or give up easily? (Fear of failure.)

2. Is my reaction to normal sex relations cold, disapproving, guilty, subject to violent revulsion afterward? (Fear of sex.)

3. Do I "suffer in silence" while feeling that people unjustly walk all over me? (Fear of self-defense.)

4. Am I careful never to depend on others? Do I believe that if I want something done I'd better do it myself? (Fear of trusting others.)

5. Am I fearful of my own thoughts? Sometimes worried by the idea that some socially unacceptable slip at the wrong time and place will ruin me? (Fear of thinking and speaking.)

6. Do I constantly seek companionship, or, when this is not available, feel lost when some sort of noise (radio, music, TV) is not present to distract me? (Fear of being alone.)

There are so many painful and damaging individual fears that it is impossible to list them all. Fear of falling, loud noises, the dark, heights, closed places, snakes, spiders, death and so on we have mentioned before. These will be all too obvious to the individual sufferer. Most of us will be amazed at the number of fears we can list. In working them out through prayer we should start with those which most strongly affect our daily life. We may be frightened stiff at the thought of going down in a submarine but, since this is highly unlikely to challenge most of us in the near future, it can be admitted and then left alone until such time as it threatens our peace of mind.

We can go a step further and state that many of the fears and anxieties from which we have suffered in the past, including specific medical diseases which worry us, have never come a step closer to us than a scarce advertisement or a morbid published or dramatized story. While believing in education and preparedness, it is actually as unnecessary to dwell on such things as it is to feed ourselves a constant diet of strawberries where a known allergy exists. Fears feed too, and wax strong on a mentally unhealthy diet. We are all allergic to fear. Yet many branches of so-called entertainment and enlightenment feed this diet to the ignorant with alarming constancy. It might be well, while fighting our battle for our impressionable children, to remember that we, too, are impressionable. The difference lies in our reputation for discrimination. If this were more in evidence in our choice as "the public" we might not have to fight Junior's battle with such violence.

Temporarily then, in waging our own crusade to free ourselves from fear, we will challenge those which seem the most overwhelming and "actual" first. As we apply prayer specifically to our more pronounced fears and confidence becomes an habitual state of mind, many of these lesser, more nebulous terrors simply fade away.

Guilt

Here again we remember that we have no intention of casting out "normal guilt." If we are to make prayer a practice in honesty we will face normal guilt and *use it* as a spur to better habits and attitudes. Abnormal guilt is invariably tied up with abnormal views on sin and an inability to believe in forgiveness. To recognize the presence of abnormal guilt we can ask ourselves:

1. Do I believe there is an "unpardonable sin," even if I cannot name it?

2. Is there a sin which I cannot personally forgive?

3. Is there anything for which I feel so deeply ashamed that I "have never mentioned it to a living soul," or never asked Divine forgiveness, or, having asked, kept repeating the request because I did not feel it should be granted?

4. Is there a given subject which I "simply refuse to discuss"?

5. Do I camouflage myself when I am with people? When I am alone? Do I pretend to feel and be things which are contrary to my nature?

Guilt, once recognized, must be matched over against love and forgiveness if we are ever to be free of it.

Inferiority Feelings

As we look at our inferiority feelings we are bound to recognize the roots of some of our defense mechanisms and telltale signs. Following the Katz and Thorpe list mentioned earlier we will question ourselves on the symptoms that indicate rather pronounced weaknesses in this emotional area:

1. Do I avoid being with others, seek to be alone rather than participate in social activities? (Seclusiveness.)

2. Am I overly reserved and easily upset in the presence of others? (Self-consciousness.)

3. Am I especially sensitive to criticism or unfavorable comparison with other persons? (Sensitiveness.)

4. Do I blame and criticize others, seeing in them the traits and motives I feel unworthy in myself? (Projection.)

5. Do I apply to myself all unfavorable remarks and criticisms made by others? (Ideas of reference.)

6. Do I try to attract attention by any method that seems likely to succeed, even if it is sometimes crude? (Attention getting.)

7. Do I try to govern others, those less successful, weaker, younger, smaller, by bullying or browbeating? (Domination.)

8. Do I cover feelings of inferiority by exaggerating a desirable tendency or trait? (Compensation.)

This is where we can usually identify whether or not we have become the silent, inhibited type, and the sooner we begin to relate ourselves to God, to our fellow man, the sooner we begin our journey back to freedom and happiness.

Hate (Misguided Love)

Here we come to the most damaging of all the demons. It is difficult to tell anyone how to evaluate their individual hostilities, resentments, dislikes, prejudices, unkindnesses. Unconsciously sensing the power of love and the penalties for distorting this power, we tend to shy away from the possibility that hatred in any form could dwell within us. But we can make a beginning and our faithfulness and intent will bring to the surface those detrimental feelings and help us rip off their disguises. We can ask:

1. Do I want to retaliate, "get even" with someone for a real or an imagined wrong?

2. Do I criticize? Build myself up by tearing others down?

3. Do I feel any satisfaction from ill-news about another, even a public figure whom I do not know? (Watch this one, it is subtle.)

4. Am I overly aggressive? (To check this you need go no farther than your daily drive in your car or trip to the market. What kind of a driver are you? Do you occupy

three lanes as your right? Advise everyone else to get off the road? Tell everyone else how to drive? At the market do you push impatiently through, grab the finest fruit practically from another's hand?)

5.   Am I ever guilty of administering "psychological torture"? Do I enjoy it even slightly? (Lest this sound like a farfetched medieval act involving manacles and chains we'd better be clear what is meant. We all have the ability to wilt the spirit of another. We use it much more often than we recognize or admit. Do we berate publicly? Humiliate? Tease? Indulge a cutting tongue? Any parent or teacher, those who deal with the young, can build up great guilt if their buried hostilities are permitted to escape in this form. Discipline and authority are fine taskmasters and, when administered justly, are rarely protested. But psychological torture with its roots in misguided love can do far more damage to others than the old birch switch.)

6.   Do I enjoy "taking people down a peg," "putting them in their place," or seeing it done to them?

These are general questions designed to indicate various facets of hatred which might be present within us. Since hostility is the most damaging and most common form which misguided love can take, and because it is not easy to identify by general questions, here is a specific test which can be taken and scored. The findings can be individually evaluated as shown at the conclusion of the test.

Here are the instructions: Read each item and then CIRCLE it either (T)   true or (F)   false:

T F   1. There seems to be less love and good will demonstrated these days.

T F   2. Those who question the authority of the Bible are looking for an excuse to do as they please.

T F   3. Even though another person's opinion makes sense to me, I prefer to make my own decisions though they may be wrong.

T F   4. I could name those responsible for the difficulty I have.

T F   5. I sometimes cheat at solitaire.

T F   6. Even though I like most people, there are those who do not accept me.

T F   7. It does upset me if people poke fun at me.

T F   8. Those around me seem to enjoy life more than I do.

T F   9. There have been times when all looked so bad that I had thoughts of taking my life.

T F 10. I gossip about my neighbors.

T F 11. My sexual relations have not been gratifying.

T F 12. Under certain conditions or circumstances I feel that racial prejudice is understandable and justified.

T F 13. Many times I feel very helpless and ineffective.

T F 14. I am suspicious of people and their actions.

T F 15. When playing cards, I would look at someone else's hand if the opportunity presented itself.

T F 16. During the day I seem to make a great number of little mistakes.

T F 17. I am a jealous person.

T F 18. I believe that children should be spanked when they disobey.

T F 19. I often find fault with people around me.

T F 20. At times my thoughts are such that I would not tell anyone about them.

T F 21. Even my loved ones misunderstand my intentions.

T F 22. I am easily annoyed by those people who do not drive properly.

T F 23. My marriage has not been as fulfilling as I would have liked.

T F 24. When a person really asks for it, I don't blame someone for giving it to them.

T F 25. I have taken things which do not belong to me.

T F 26. I am frequently annoyed by pets.

T F 27. I am sometimes sarcastic to people around me.

T F 28. I am frequently bothered by head- or stomach-aches.

T F 29. Personality tests are not as valid as some would have you believe.

T F 30. When someone has wronged me I feel like getting even with them.

Left Score ———   Right Score ———

Now score the test in the following way: Look at items 5, 10, 15, 20, 25, 30. If any of these statements are marked "false," merely count them and write the number at the bottom of the test on the left-hand side.

For all the other statements on the test, count those marked "true" and write this total at the bottom of the test on the right-hand side.

We are testing only two (2) factors or traits on this test. The two numbers at the bottom of the test represent these two factors.

The number on the left is to determine how honest you have been. If the number is 4 or above, you have not been honest with yourself. Read these items again carefully and evaluate them in the light of your past experience. Try to determine how you *honestly* feel—not the way you think you *ought* to feel. If the number is 3 or less it is safe to assume that you have answered the other statements with a fair degree of honesty.

The number on the right-hand side indicates the degree of hostility (hate) you possess, whether you realize this or not. All people possess hostility. It is the degree or amount that determines the consequences. It is more detrimental if you are not aware that this is within you.

Evaluation of Your Hostility Score
(For those with an honesty score of 3 or less.)

0-8	9-16	17-24
Not strong	Average	Strong

Evaluation of Your Hostility Score
(For those with an honesty score of 4 or more.)

The previous scale is not appropriate here. It can be meaningful only when you are honest on the test. Now take it again and see how honest you can be. Let this be a challenge. This is a great opportunity for you to learn and grow and move toward freedom. "The *Truth* will make you free."

Human beings learn quite early to "suppress," or to restrain their aggressive behavior from being expressed overtly, that is, outwardly, particularly toward others. We must keep in mind that if these aggressive feelings are held in, this does not mean that we have gotten rid of them. We may disguise these feelings. We may deny them. We may delay them. We may even substitute other feelings in their place. This does not mean that we have *destroyed* them.

It is a rare person indeed who will find no misguided love in their inner kingdom, so do not cringe even momentarily from what you find within yourself. If we can admit it, we have taken the first, great step.

We now *Look Outward* and regard our present environment as objectively and honestly as we know how. We ask: How do other people treat me and why? Do I think people talk about me? (Inferiority Feelings) Do I run myself down, "fish" for compliments? (More Inferiority Feelings) Do I talk all the time? (Guilt and Inferiority) Do I find it difficult to express myself at all? Am I so afraid to be labeled a "poor sport" that I will go along with anything and sacrifice my own convictions?

We recognize our demons in our relationship to others and then ask "why?" For each the problems and the answers as to "why" we respond as we do will be individual but the object is to get to the root of the matter so we know specifically what we are surrendering.

The last direction in which the compass points is *Onward,* not to peer into the future with a crystal ball, but to gain a positive concept of ourselves as we would like to be. We can *always* go beyond what we are today and forward motion is growth. As we look onward, we recognize the fact that "conditions" are the one thing we know which both *are,* and *are not.* They "are" only until some force changes them, and in this case the force will be our own new direction. That direction is established, the blueprint drawn as we look to what we wish to become. This is not idle daydreaming. Behind it is the active conviction of its possibility. We are dealing with mighty forces day in and day out. It is up to us to use or to pervert them. Once we understand this, tomorrow can find us a step nearer our ideal.

Meeting the Demands of Life

Thus far we have regarded our defense mechanisms, looked for telltale signs of inner unrest, recognized the three areas in which we can find weaknesses and decided to evaluate each separately, our aim to develop a proper balance between the emotional, social and intellectual parts of our nature until we are integrated or whole personalities. We have looked Backward, Inward, Outward and Onward. There is yet one important phase to be regarded.

How do we meet the demands of life?

This is a question of responses. Certain demands are placed upon each one of us daily. Some we welcome, from some of them we shrink, but there they are. The chief point is how do we react to them and why? Do we keep trying to change the external factors or have we begun to grasp the idea that the first change must come within ourselves?

Actually it is not so important *what* happens as *how* it *affects us.* We will never run out of problems. To the balanced person each problem is a challenge, an opportunity that he must work out and the fact is that he will react with less grief, anguish, pain to even the most humanly difficult situation than the unbalanced individual.

Two men lose good, steady jobs. To one this spells defeat and he talks a great deal about what might-have-been but does nothing. To the other it is a temporary gap to be filled with new opportunities. He goes onward. Two men lose their life's savings. One jumps from a window. The other takes work in a gas station and continues to enjoy family, friends, self-respect and an optimism concerning the future. Two women lose their husbands through sudden death. One gives up, goes into a "decline," accepts self-pity, becomes morbid. Her family disintegrates and her children suffer. The other knows the extreme sadness of loss, but keeps her balance, holds her home together, meets the responsibilities and obligations of every day.

To evaluate how we personally meet life's demands we need to ask more questions: *What is my relationship to myself?* Do I now accept myself as I am, strengths and weaknesses, knowing that the power to "balance my budget" is at hand? Do I insult God by rating myself too low? Do I constantly place limitations on myself? *Do I wish I were someone else?*

How do I relate myself to others? Do I fear them? Feel superior to them? Feel inferior to them?

How do I relate myself to my daily life? Do I recognize my problems and deal with them the best way I know how? Do I hide them from myself? Do I attack my work with worry, dread, lack of confidence? Do I dread coming home to my family? Leaving the family circle for business or social functions?

How do I start the day? Am I grumpy, discouraged when I get up? And at bedtime, do I find I have a "busy head" and cannot go to sleep? Do I attempt to escape my responsibilities with illnesses, too much social life, too much reading or entertainment? Do I permit confusion to defeat me, where I have so much to do I never get *anything* done? Do I face every task as a "chore" and grit my teeth and overdo it? Am I so compulsive that I can't stand a thing out of place, a speck of dirt, a sudden change in plans? Am I so disorganized that my work is never well done?

How do I relate myself to God? Am I a supplicant? A miserable sinner? A total stranger? A distant relative? Or do I actually believe he is Our Father, "closer than breathing, nearer than hands and feet"?

When we have honestly evaluated our defense mechanisms, our telltale symptoms, the areas in which we need help, the state of our inner kingdom and how we meet the demands of life we have made our initial effort toward self-honesty. We should know ourselves consciously as we have never done before. We have accomplished the preliminary step to prayer and should have the insight necessary to begin at once to apply Prayer Therapy as outlined in the next chapter and see the change it can bring to our lives.

13

PRAYER THERAPY ON A DAILY BASIS

OUR TOUR OF EVALUATION IS NOW COMPLETE. WE have surveyed our heights, depths, present shortcomings and limitations, our unlimited potential.

What next?

The first thing required is the Clean Up Operation. Recognition itself has disarmed our defense mechanisms. They will never again be able to completely deceive us. The intent to be honest, because truth is of God, has the whole power of the universe behind it. From now on we will see clearly.

We affirm this. We accept it.

Next, our telltale signs have served their purpose. They have forced us to ask "why?"——what is causing my depression, psychosomatic symptoms, self-righteousness? And "where," in what area of my "self," does this cause lie? *We now drop these symptoms entirely. They are never to be carried into our prayers.*

The reason is obvious. The pain occasioned by a broken arm is a definite warning that there is something amiss. If we concentrate on treating the pain instead of locating the fracture we will not set the broken bone. In that case the pain has no choice but to stay with us.

Our telltale signs are on the pain level. Once we have accepted their warning, asked "why" and "where," and set to work to correct the cause, we can rest assured that they will disappear. The symptom has no power to *cause* anything.

We recognize this. We let the symptom go.

Rebuilding a Harmonious Kingdom

This brings us to the world of actual causes as we have located them—within ourselves. We have looked backward. Now we flood our past with understanding and forgiveness. We release ourselves and others from any blame, any condemnation. Until we consciously do this the past can make unconscious slaves of us. The only way we can successfully release our past is to place ourselves, this precise minute, under the law of Love, *make up our minds* to enter Love's Circle and comply with the two commandments of Jesus. From that exact moment the past, its limitations, memories, mistakes, *has no power in our lives today*.

We have left the nets that enmeshed us to follow Him and keep His commandments. This is true repentance.

Now we look to our demons. These too can and must be disarmed. The process will come more easily if we see them for what they truly are, distortions of the feelings and emotions God meant man to have. They are the other side of the coin, the destructive against the constructive, the negative against the positive. If we match the human distortion against the God-quality we can see this plainly.

Guilt	*Forgiveness*
Hate	*Love*
Inferiority Feelings	*Confidence*
Fear	*Faith*
Victim	*Victor*

The Christian, Christ's man, is *Victor,* not *Victim.* Thus the Christian can turn confidently in prayer to dispel whatever has been keeping him in bondage. Such a desire is in line with the Law of Love, hence with the Divine Will.

Exactly where and how do we begin?

We tackle *first things first.* We apply specific Prayer Therapy wherever we feel our greatest need. Looking at the task of rebuilding consciousness as a Whole might prove overwhelming. But we bear in mind what any good gardener or housewife or architect knows. You cannot weed, plant, water a "whole" garden. Nor clean a "whole" house. Nor build a "whole" city. The "whole" is the objective in our mind's eye. *Doing* it, however, is a question of weeding a rose bed, watering a lawn. Or cleaning the kitchen and moving on to a single bedroom. Or setting one brick upon another to construct the Town Hall. The end result will be a beautiful garden, a clean house, an entire city. Its accomplishment is a question of intelligent and loving daily application.

We ourselves will work out our salvation on orderly progression, which is another way of saying that Patience will have her perfect work with us. To insist on miracles is to invite defeat through discouragement. Miracles *do* happen but so far as we yet know they are outside our realm of positive expectation. In the past they have not been dependable nor repeatable. Prayer Therapy has.

The Prayer Therapy method is to start with one facet, stay with it for a week, then move on to something else. We follow our individual blueprint as laid out in our individual evaluation. Regardless of what inharmony we seek to change, however, the technique will be the same:

1.   We recognize a God of Love *within us* as the healing and directing power of our lives.

2.   We consciously surrender any negative quality (motive, drive, thought, feeling) we do not want.

3.   We invite God's power to fill the void our surrender has created.

4.   In specific times of prayer and throughout our day we hold positive, healthful, wholesome thoughts and images, certain that these *alone* are in line with God's will for his offspring.

5.   When we pray we believe that we have received the specific help we have requested—and we *act* as though we had received it.

6.   We meditate on God as *Love,* on Jesus' Commandments to *love,* and seek entrance to that Circle of Perfection . . . love of God, of self as God's child, of neighbor as self.

7. We *listen,* wait for a sense of Victory, a feeling of Presence, that tells us, "I AM here. ALL IS well."

8. It is done. Glory to God in the highest. *We give thanks!*

If we faithfully follow this technique, in the end we cannot fail. Why? Because God cannot fail. If we *surrender* the negative, the destructive, the distortion, and then *accept* the positive, our victory is assured. It cannot be otherwise. God cannot withhold Good. It is against His nature. Then what is wanted is that we unblock—and receive. Forgiveness, love, confidence, faith will flow to us from an ever-present inexhaustible source if we can only get ourselves out of the way.

Breaking Old Habit

"If we can get ourselves out of the way."

The first time we discussed this in a Prayer Therapy class one red-headed chap said disgustedly, "IF, there's always an 'if.' Even in an academic experiment you leave a loophole, an escape hatch in case the thing doesn't work."

That's a perfectly logical objection. But "The Thing" does work and the "Ifs" are dependent on perfectly avoidable traps. Since pitfalls do exist, however, it is only fair to put them on our daily chart so we won't fall in.

It is true that we don't take our symptoms into prayer, nor focus our attention on them. We get at the cause, apply our prayer technique to that cause for one week, "believing that we have received."

And then, some sunny Thursday of the following week or a month from Sunday we find ourselves manifesting the same old symptoms. We are depressed, overcome with anxiety. Or we want to get away from everyone and hide. Or we arrive home shaken and out of sorts to realize that we have driven through Sunday traffic with resentment on the throttle and aggression at the wheel. Hate, guilt, fear, or inferiority feelings have not only threatened, but carried the day.

Are we a failure? Is God a failure? Is Prayer Therapy a Valentine philosophy, pretty to eye and ear, but not much on application? Unless we understand the danger and know what to do about it, the very least that can happen is that we will be discouraged, doubt our principle. If we are despondent enough, having "tried so hard" we may even feel like Job who simply couldn't understand, after he'd been a "good man" all his life, why so many afflictions were visited on him. His first idea was simply to "curse God and die."

Job was an extremist but then so are many of us. So it is better that we understand what has happened to us. Actually it is an old story in Christian progression. We remember Paul's complaint: "For the good that I would, I do not: but the evil which I would not, that I do."

He points out that he "delights in the law of God after the inward man: (He is trying to live by the commandments of Love) But I see another law in my members, warring against the law of my mind . . ."

Now what possible law could go on warring in the *members* once we had tried to establish God's law in our minds?

The answer is *habit*. The self we must get out of the way is our conditioned, habitual "old" self.

Paul himself answered this when he added, "Now if I do that I would not, *it is no more I that do it. . . .*"

The seed is sown, our will open to the Divine healing power, but old responses and thought patterns which are no longer *us* keep trying to reassert themselves. We speak of the "force of habit." Here we are dealing with that force. A habit is "an aptitude or inclination for some action (or reaction) acquired by repetition and showing itself in facility of performance or in decreased resistance." It becomes involuntary. Reflex action.

If it has been acquired by repetition, even after new patterns are sown, it may require repeated dismissal before it expends all its "force." We gave it the force, and we can take it away. But we do not do so by suppressing it. We supplant it.

Thus the first question we ask is: *Are we still trying*

to change the external factor? In many of us this is the deep-rooted "habit" that must be surrendered before anything else. If we are trying to change such "bad habits" as quarreling, grumbling, temper, drinking (and with our children, thumb sucking, bed-wetting) by saying "Let's have a little will power. Let's grow up," we need look no further for the self we must get out of the way. We are still trying to suppress a symptom rather than alter the cause.

Once more let us be clear on this. Unhappy people build up tensions and the "habit" is a release, a symptom. What requires correcting is the *need*. A new release. The moment the symptom reasserts itself we must instantly recognize the cause. That is the new habit that is required. To resist dealing with the external factor.

Then our help is at hand. We can say with Paul, " 'It is no more I that do it . . . for I have chosen the law of God after the inward man.' I have chosen a *new* release. I identify myself with the law-abiding Spirit of the Universe and all my releases are expressions of that."

This is first aid when undesirable symptoms try to reassert themselves. Resist dealing with the symptoms. Let love dictate your releases. This applies to giving help to your children. Since love has placed them in your care, you can confidently ask that light be given you on the cause of any tensions, and that you be inspired to show the child a *new* release. The very fact that more love, more harmony will be present in your home through your own spiritual progress will often do wonders to release the tensions in your child. Tensions do not long remain where Love's healing power is flowing freely.

Supposing we have already reversed our tendency to try to change the external factor, and still the undesirable symptom persists. Ask yourself another question: *"Am I living the problem rather than the answer?"*

This is not nearly as farfetched as it sounds. It can be very subtle too, because we are often unaware that we are doing it. The problem belongs to the past. The *answer* is here today. We would have no trouble in living the answer if we had thoroughly released the past.

Let us take the case of a wife who had discovered that her husband had been unfaithful. He admitted it, said he was truly sorry, and assured her that his true desire was to begin to live immediately a happier, better adjusted, perfectly faithful life with her and their children. This was his answer to a difficult situation, his true desire, and he was prepared to begin to live that answer at once. She, as the "injured party," had to make the choice. Seeking her own answer and true desire, she decided to remain with him. It took her some time to make up her mind and, during that time, the problem had become a habit. She wanted her happy marriage, but she would not live the answer. She kept living the problem, neither forgiving nor refraining from reminding him daily of his defection.

She wished "everything to be the way it was before," and right there the wife cheated herself by dishonesty. We cannot climb back and alter the past. All we can do is to view it with understanding and forgiveness—and release it. She had a perfect right to choose to live alone. Or to choose to remain. But once the choice was made the only way Love could heal the breach was for them both to let yesterday go, to break the hold of the problem by accepting the answer—and living it.

Her household displayed every symptom of a house divided against itself—quarreling, recriminations, tensions, and tears for all—and God himself could do nothing about it until she recognized that an answer *eliminates* a problem, but that we must accept and live the answer if it is to be of any benefit to us.

We recognize as abnormal people who have lived and died in poverty and rags with many thousands of dollars hidden in tin cans in their miserable dwellings. Supply and abundance were at hand but somewhere they had formed the habit of poverty, and the symptoms persisted.

We compound our own difficulties, make life very trying for ourselves, even make our own happiness an impossibility when we refuse our answers and continue to clutch our problems.

If we will consciously stop trying to change the external factor, and begin today to live in today's answer, we will break the hold of the past, and deprive the habits of yesterday of their force. This is the only way to starve those symptoms which seem to have their roots in strong, oft-repeated thought patterns which are no longer "ours," but memory pictures of the "old" man which we have put off through prayer.

Establishing New Patterns

There will be many hours in our day when we are not at actual prayer. But we will be thinking, imagining, planning, reacting, talking to ourselves.

Before we began to apply Prayer Therapy this may have seemed unimportant. Now we know that it is not. We have discovered that what gets our attention gets us. If the frame of mind we have sought in prayer is not kept in focus we will find that Love is getting possibly one-fourteenth of our waking time, and we are very apt to spend the rest (by far the greater portion) of our day permitting our old "habitual" feelings to dictate to us.

Our safety lies in forming new and healthful patterns. We will have God's help. But we must cooperate. This does not mean panting and straining and making a great effort. It means relaxation and a conviction that Love attends us in all our ways.

This can become an habitual state of mind, our involuntary reaction. Until it does we must be alert. *We must delay our habitual, old responses, insist on the new reaction we want on the spot.* We don't wait to pray about it later. We act instantly each time the old pattern would reassert itself.

It will take practice. Persistent repetition has formed our unwanted patterns and habits. Now we will be persistent in re-forming them, reeducating our subconscious.

The old injunction to count ten before an attack of temper was a perfectly sound method of delaying responses. But without insisting on the desired reaction, it would be possible to use those seconds to simply think up meaner things to say, and then it would serve no purpose.

It is perfectly legitimate to count ten or use any other trick in the pack if it helps us to establish these all important new habits. One couple who came to Prayer Therapy classes had tremendous difficulty overcoming nagging quarrels which had become habitual with them over twenty years of marriage. In their direct prayer they applied themselves to an understanding of love, decided that quarreling was a symptom of something amiss, and then they worked out a method for delaying their responses and insisting on a new reaction.

"We know we love each other," the husband reasoned. "So why quarrel?"

They decided that both suffered a good deal from nameless tensions, that when they quarreled they were not verbalizing anything exact. In fact in the process they completely lost touch with themselves and each other so that the chances were they fought about "nothing" and this had simply become their usual if unpleasant way of letting off steam.

"We agreed not to stem 'the free flow of opinions or ideas,'" the husband reported, "or to suppress any valid argument which might air out a difficulty. But we would delay our responses and insist that our argument made sense by rephrasing everything the other had said before we replied to it."

In other words, his wife had to take his statement and say "If I understand what you mean, you mean thus and so. . . ." Then she would reply to it and he would say "If I understand what you mean, you said this and that." In delaying their responses they shortly discovered that neither understood what the other said at all and wound up in helpless laughter when the reason became clear. Neither was actually saying *anything*.

Let us say right here that laughter is one of the best reactions we can insist on when we are dealing with ourselves. If we can get to the point where we are honestly amused by the temptation to a negative response, the only possible reason is that we have seen it for what it is, a distortion. We then know that we have had a glimpse of reality and regained our sense of proportion.

The only reason that our image in those alarming mirrors at the Fun House of an amusement park does not frighten us is because we *know* what we truly look like and do not for a minute believe that this creature with a stomach as wide as an elephant and a head like a pin is *us*.

The specific things upon which we are working by applied Prayer Therapy must be protected throughout the day by instant insistence on the reaction we have asked and received. But there are small things that we may not wish to tackle directly for many months which can often be overcome by this simple method of establishing a new habit of thought about it as we go along. Driving our car is an interesting place to experiment. Or doing the dishes. Or getting the children up for school in the morning. Or the barking of a neighbor's dog.

We know what our past response has been. All right. The next time the situation arises, challenge it! Delay a moment and, instead of permitting the habit to control us, state definitely that you are *not* annoyed, or angry, or flustered. You *are* in control and you *are* serene, unhurried, relaxed. You can even insist that you are amused. Or joyous. And this response will become automatic—the genuine one.

This is not a question of self-will or will power. It can only be accomplished if it is based on a conviction that a God of Love has willed this state of mind from the beginning and we are finally cooperating with that Will. It is a very gentle, calm realigning of ourselves with *right action* and the *right reaction* of all living things to the harmony and laws of Love. It is a simple question of making a choice. But since the false choice has become habitual, we must persist until the pattern is changed and all its power of suggestion destroyed.

Such new attitudes on your part may well heal the whole situation. If it does not, it is bound to heal your response to it and leave you a happier, healthier individual.

14

ONWARD AND UPWARD

IN DEALING WITH THE FOUR DEMONS WE HAVE BEEN reeducating the emotional self. One prayer period a day should be set aside for this specific purpose. If we follow the outlined steps, when we next reevaluate ourselves and look inward we should find a great change for the better.

Ten Steps Toward a Richer, Fuller Life

There are other things we can do, however, to improve the manner in which we meet the demands of life, increase our joy, keep our growth constant and balanced. Each of them has its own special place in our development and if we are going to try one, it is only fair to try them all.

1. *Pray the last thing at night before going to sleep.* The subconscious does not sleep. God does not sleep. If we turn to Him with love and confidence after we have closed our eyes, we, however, *will* sleep, and will gain a rest and refreshment from the night better than any we have ever known. Brother Lawrence, a gentle and saintly monk of the 17th century, wrote: "Those whose spirits are stirred by the breath of the Holy Spirit go forward even in sleep." This is both true and a present possibility for each of us if we will turn our last waking thought to Him and invite the Holy Spirit to be present

with us throughout the night. If God is minding our business, could it be in better hands? If Love is feeding our subconscious while our body and conscious mind rest, we will find the time of sleep a growing period and a source of true repose.

2. *Pray the first thing in the morning.* We can train ourselves, as soon as consciousness returns with the morning, to give our first moment, even before opening our eyes, to the awareness of God. We will not dread the day, be a pre-coffee growler, if each morning as we awaken we say and try to feel, "This is the day that the Lord hath made. Let us rejoice and be glad in it." We consciously reestablish our awareness of our partnership with the Almighty. Then we can arise with true expectations of good throughout the day.

3. *Pray for the world.* The growth of our Social Self depends on our relationship to the world in which we live, and how we discharge our responsibilities to the whole. Some of us carry the material side of this responsibility almost feverishly and feel very ineffectual because our sphere of usefulness does not go further. Others feel helpless, shrug, and do nothing. What *can* we do, they ask, about national problems, world problems, wars and rumors of wars, *isms* and *ologies,* except to cast our little vote and work in our own backyard?

We forget that we have a spiritual responsibility and that prayer power, being infinite, knows not great or small, near or far. We can and should support our leaders with our prayers. We can affirm that God reigns, that "the government is upon His shoulders." We can think of all the people of the world and say, "Our Father." Then we will begin to know what Brotherhood means. Ten righteous men, says the Bible, could save a town. We have no way of knowing what we could accomplish if each of us gave our righteous prayers daily to the world.

4. *Prayer for others.* Our relationship to other people is a most important part of our daily life as we found in our evaluation when we looked outward. While we cannot and should not attempt to change others, or remold

them according to our will, there is something we can do which still leaves each man his freedom of choice.

The story is told of two psychiatrists whose offices were in the same building. Each morning they rode up together in the same elevator, the short psychiatrist to the 4th floor, the tall psychiatrist to the 9th floor. They had never met, yet each morning as they rode upward together the short psychiatrist looked up and spat on the other, who took no notice. Eventually the elevator operator could stand it no longer. After letting the short psychiatrist out on four, she turned to the other and said, "That man spits on you every day. Why don't you *do* something?" "Why should I?" he replied. "It's not *my* problem."

This is only half the truth, however. Had the tall psychiatrist known anything of the healing power of prayer, he would have known we always have the right and privilege of praying for the other fellow. This is *not* an attempt to coerce him or make him conform to our will, but of seeing him according to God's will, without problems, Love's child, whole and perfect. Here we release love's healing power for another, love our neighbor as ourself. This art perfected by Jesus cast out devils, raised up invalids, eliminated sins.

5.   *Pray for our enemies.* This was a specific injunction by the Master Prayer, and Jesus said we should forgive before making our own gifts at the altar. It would be deceitful at this point to say we can love all people equally. Some people just aren't very lovable. The trick in praying for those who do us injury is to separate the sin from the sinner. We can and should hate the sin. We can forgive the sinner.

When the woman taken in adultery was brought before Jesus he did not condone the act. In fact he told her plainly not to do it again. But he forgave the woman. He didn't "condemn" her, hold the sin against her. His forgiveness healed. Not once but many times. We are all in need of this healing forgiveness. Until we learn to forgive, however, we will not be able to accept it fully. Why? Because we know that what is true of one must be true of all. We claim this blessing for ourselves and our loved ones, but we know he is "Our Father." If we are able to expect forgiveness so is every other child of God.

Only Love is strong enough to forgive and if we deny our own forgiveness to anyone, are we not denying Love's presence within us? Where then is our healing power? It is not functioning because we have blocked it. So if we wish to make progress we had better begin to forgive immediately. The demands of life include a healthy relationship to others.

The act of forgiveness does not start with outward display. We do not have to treat everyone alike. Jesus did not make a disciple out of the adulteress after forgiving her. Quietly, within our own heart, we turn the individual we have called "enemy" over to God. We release them and ourselves of damaging emotions under the Law of Love. If the other man does not accept his freedom as yet, there is nothing more we can do. But in keeping the Commandments ourselves we rise above a very dangerous situation and can approach the altar with a purer heart.

6. *Ask ourselves daily what we truly desire.* Words give impulse to thought. Thought gives impulse to prayer. It has been hard and bitter to accept the fact that whatever condition we are in, we have chosen it. Again we face the fact that what gets our attention gets us. So if we desire something different, we must be specific and consistent on that point. Do we truly desire abundant supply? Confidence? Security? Harmony? Health? Very well. Choose them. Entertain them. Think on them. Identify with them. These are our true desires now. We are looking onward, and it is only as we inspect our desires, bring the ones we wish into focus, that our prayers can become positive. This step will determine the direction of our future growth.

7. *Each day try at some period to be honestly alone with self and God.* Honestly alone means more than putting aside your book, even the Good Book, or your knitting or turning off the TV. It means setting aside busy thoughts. In this meditation time you will not bring any

problems or demons or anything of "this world." It is here, and here only, that you can improve your understanding of God and your relationship to Him. Here you truly try to sense the Presence within. We can start with a well-loved prayer or Bible phrase and then let ourselves ponder it, feel its meaning. If we fail on this step we will always remain something of a "fox hole" prayer, believing that we only go to God with a problem to be resolved. In this period we go only for God Himself and for a better acquaintance with Him.

8. *Each day try at least once to be consciously with people (or one person).* This means to be aware of someone else and his needs. It means trying to give yourself away. You will not, in this period, be aware of yourself— no fair thinking how others are reacting to you, how you look to them, whether they are noticing our intelligence, or our love, or our spirituality. When we first try this we find that too much of our relationship to others has very little to do with *them* except as they react to *us*. This is to be *self-*centered. To give ourselves away is to be *love-*centered.

9. *Determine daily in one specific area to affect your environment instead of reflecting it.* A mature, integrated person, secure in his relationship to God, does not sit back and, like the chameleon, reflect the choices others have made, their thoughts, or the tensions and confusions in their surroundings. It was E. Stanley Jones who said that, if we concentrate on what others think, we are not a voice but an echo.

Every one of us has had the experience of being at a party which seemed either a deadly bore or a bedlam of ferocious arguments. Suddenly some one person will come into the room. Their good cheer and genuine bubbling spirit can lift the party to its feet and set another keynote (and we do not refer to a jokester going into an act, but to some quality or state of mind in the newcomer), or a calm, sensible, authoritative person will weld the bedlam of argument, dismiss it, and suddenly we are all talking happily about our common interests. Oil has been poured on troubled waters.

How do they do it? They have simply affected the environment around them in a constructive way instead of sitting back and taking on the pattern already established. Each of us has the power to do this in both large and small ways. What we need is to stop being an echo, search out true desires, and then put them into action.

One of our Prayer Therapy students was having great trouble with his mother-in-law. When he came home from work each afternoon he found her always at fever pitch, angry, complaining, accusing. The young man didn't bear it in meek silence (which would have been suppressing something without uprooting it and bad enough) but reflected her mood like a shiny mirror. This was equally futile. If she complained that she and her daughter had too much work to do what with all the children and all the laundry, he griped right back about how hard he worked at the office. If she grew sarcastic and accused him of not making enough money, up went his voice as he informed her that he made more than the average but she and her daughter could have broken Rockefeller. Each degree of anger in her met an exact correspondence in him, an echo, not a voice. The wife, caught in the middle, yelled first on one side and then another. The children just yelled.

"I truly desire peace," he told the class.

They discussed who was setting the tempo in the household and he agreed that it was his mother-in-law. He was simply reflecting whatever mood she established. "Next time she complains, tell her you're sorry," someone suggested.

"But I'm not," he said.

"However, you desire peace, harmony. You have to be the one to initiate the change. You take control of the situation and keep insisting by your answers that this is the way you wish your environment to be . . . You want it to be courteous. Well, you be courteous. Half the environment becomes so instantly."

The first time he said, "I'm sorry," he robbed his mother-in-law of speech. The dictation of the scene had changed hands. Eventually he was able to establish the pattern he wanted by refusing to reflect what went on, and determining to affect it by his own conduct.

10. *Each day say a definite "no" to some activity, and a definite "yes" to another.* Almost every student who studied Prayer Therapy spoke wistfully at one time or another of simplifying life. Doubtless many of us should do some simplifying if we are to maintain physical and mental peace. We live the pace that killeth. Simplification, however, is not necessarily a question of doing less, gaining more leisure, or even resting more. Labor saving devices have given most of us less hard labor than any previous generation, yet more of us suffer from nervous exhaustion.

It isn't that we work too hard. It is that we scatter our forces. We feel unconsciously guilty if we say "no" to any worthy demand, yet our "yes" is too often unconsidered and indiscriminate. We tend to take on not too much activity, but too many activities, then rush feverishly from one to another supported by good intentions and nerves, nowhere giving of our best. We feel frustrated, overburdened, and no wonder. More and more it is a question of too much leisure thoughtlessly occupied.

During the war civilian drivers were challenged everywhere by a sign which read: Is This Trip Necessary? Many of them have insisted that they were amazed to find how many times the true answer was "no" and how relieved they were when this simple question ended much fruitless dashing about. "Of course, we had to think and plan to get the necessaries done." one woman told me. "But once you got the hang of it, it was amazing how much nicer it was not to be on the go all the time."

We no longer have to question whether such things are absolutely necessary. But we would get immediate relief from confusion if we did learn to ask, Is this for me? My talent and taste? Have I the time? Can I accept an office with the PTA and work with a Girl Scout Troop as well? Or, since our fourth child arrived only a few months ago and my husband is working nights, is it necessary to make all new curtains for the living room?

Many husbands complain, not of the cost or inconvenience of things, but with the certainty that Mother is over-extending and he and the children will suffer. Can a man who is already serving on the church board and managing a Little League ball team also play in the office golf tournament on the week-end of a board supper without becoming a nervous wreck or snapping off his best pitcher's or a good client's head?

There is our chosen work, our family life, all with a priority. Our prayer times should be sacred not from superstition but because we cannot give what we have not got, and we need periods for personal enrichment and growth as well as a serene foundation for our activities.

Something has got to go. We must learn to regard our life as a whole and to say "no" to the things we cannot truthfully fit into the picture, no matter how pleasant or worthwhile they might be as an isolated activity. We have to give ourselves a break. Nor is this selfish. It does not deny the need to give ourselves away, but the foolishness in scattering our goods. It is being realistic to see that we do others an injustice when we do half a job, or do one under pressure and tension.

Where we decide to say our "no" will be governed by our sense of values. I know a young mother who was verging on collapse because she felt that with three young children, an income so modest that no labor saving devices were available, membership on her church altar society, a husband who worked odd hours, she was still not giving enough time to her children. It drove her wild that she was never able to sit with them in a recollected fashion and read or play games.

She lived in Hartford, Connecticut, and one evening her own mother called from New York and caught the girl in tears. "Here I am," she sobbed, "five-thirty at night, and I haven't gotten to my dusting or vacuuming yet."

"Do you remember when you were a little girl, this used to be our reading time?" the mother asked.

The girl sobbed harder. "I do. Oh, I do. I wish I was there now."

"But what you don't remember, because you didn't even notice, was that I swept the dust under the rug or just let it lay some nights so we could have our reading time. What do you think is more important for you and your children?"

That is the question. What is important? If we find that the reading time means more to our family, they will have to exist with a bit of excess dust. We must simply say "no" to the vacuum cleaner and then, with complete good cheer, sweep the dust under the rug. There may be groans from those housewives whose choice lies in providing that floor you can eat from. But if this is not your choice, are you a voice or an echo?

Even when the call seems to be of a religious or Christian nature we must still examine it. As the wise Quaker, Thomas Kelly, pointed out, we cannot die on every cross. Nor should we try. If we do not honestly believe we can undertake a thing and give it all it deserves, we must say "no." It does not put God on the spot. God's work will not go undone simply because you have already assumed all you can faithfully discharge today. Perhaps your neighbor has not undertaken her full share and will not be asked to if good old Jane will just take it on. You have no right to deprive her of her opportunity to serve, or to doubt her willingness and ability to do so. If it is God's work, someone will be found, you may be sure.

We can begin by saying "no" to the trivia we all would recognize as completely unnecessary if we ever thought about it. We will gain judgment and confidence as we go, but if we would live a simpler life, we should begin today.

When we have begun to say a considered "no" we can, from the same premise, say a considered "yes." Once daily we can begin to give our full consent to some activity. This is very different from our usual agreement which is often automatic or hedged with reluctance, resentment, reserves. We are asked to dinner or to make a speech sometime next month. Carelessly, because it's pleasanter and easier, and also because it seems so far off a lot of things can happen, we agree. When the time rolls around we wonder what could have possessed us. Or some friend calls and says, "What are you doing Sunday week?" and we innocently reply, "Nothing." Whereupon we are asked to serve on a committee to Beautify the Bandstand in the Park, and are caught with "nothing" upon which to base our "no." One very busy writer of my acquaintance, who had to learn to value her consent, took to asking quite bluntly, "What did you have in mind?" And we have a perfect right to do the same before we feel trapped into reluctant acquiescence.

To consciously say "yes," on the other hand, is to throw all our powers and talents and concentration behind the elected activity. It is the positive prelude to accomplishment and unifies us with the creative Spirit from the first, whether it is cleaning a house, writing a poem, taking the children on a picnic, or building a shelf for the kitchen. If we bake a careless cake or give a half-hearted speech, it were better for us and for others that it had not been done at all. But if we throw our positive agreement behind the project we will be amazed at the speed, perfection, and joy with which it can be accomplished. No "buts." No feelings that we should be doing something else, even something harder, nobler. No. "I have thought about this, and now I choose to do it with my whole heart." Each of us will truly find a hidden storehouse of power pouring through if we clear the channels by giving our full consent.

The Perfect Man

We tend to shy away from thoughts of perfection. Nothing, we say, is perfect. Or, nothing in this world is perfect. Yet this nothing, or this thing we have never encountered, is a standard we all seem to know about. It must exist somewhere, must be something. It is impossible to think, talk about or strive for nothing. Try it if you don't believe me!

God, we may say, is perfect. This recognition that there is such a thing as perfection must then be an awareness granted by God within us. All our movements are a yearning toward our present understanding of perfection. Health is more perfect to us than illness. Intelligence more perfect than stupidity. Love (even with our present slight understanding of the word) more perfect than hate. Plenty more perfect than want. Hence we might say, they are more God-like. And each of us, to the limit of our present understanding, strives for something better, more perfect, more God-like, than we have yet known.

Over and over spiritual leaders have said that, if we could forget ourselves, we could become a better transparency for God's perfection.

The difficulty here is that we cannot forget ourselves by an *act of will*. We can project our voice, raise our hand, put an X in a precise square but, by an act of will, we cannot suddenly get ourselves off our hands. The more we try to forget self the more we are apt to have self on our mind.

In our evaluating, applying Prayer Therapy to the inner kingdom, we might suspect the danger of developing a self-centeredness. We could, if we concentrated on this self rather than simply evaluating it, run the risk of self-condemnation, even self-hatred.

There is a way, however, by which we can have absolute protection against self-centeredness, or self-hatred. It is an important step in our wistful yearning toward perfection.

We must concentrate on seeing in ourselves the person Jesus sees in us.

Not the person others see in us. Not the person we have seen in ourselves. But the person we are capable of becoming when we recognize the potential with which God has endowed each one of us, and start releasing that person.

When we turn our attention to what Jesus sees in us, we start working out the pattern of our life as we were intended to live it. As this new person we are *becoming*

(not a dream figure or a might-have-been) we find ourselves doing things quite beyond our previous capacity
simply because we have aligned ourselves with the resources of the Infinite which are now at our disposal.
Our faith then is not passive. Our direction is not inward. Life is lived daringly with the challenge to become this new person. Such high adventure will not
permit us to become introspective. If we daily try to see
in ourselves the person Jesus sees in us already we are
looking onward, upward, and *traveling* in that direction.
This is our perspective. We cannot lose it.

What does Jesus see in us? How can we be sure he
does not regard us as miserable sinners? Much of his
ministry was given to teaching repentance (changing our
minds) and the remission of sins. Our Prayer Therapy
has helped us to understand this, accept it, and become
his followers. In studying to live by his commandments
of love we bring ourselves even closer. But other important parts of his teaching included telling us the truth
about the perfect Father-God. And the truth about the
perfect Son-Man.

He was able to give this enlarged vision of self to
those about him during his life on earth and he continued
to give it to those who would accept it after his ascension.

Let us look at Matthew, the publican, a collector of
taxes. The word "publican" was always associated with
some other derogatory word. "Publicans and sinners,"
"publicans and harlots." Jesus saw in Matthew something
more than the neighbors saw, something more than Matthew himself saw. He saw him as one of the foundation
stones of a great new movement that would change the
course of history. When Matthew began to concentrate
on what Jesus saw in him, new doors opened, old barriers disappeared, and he moved into a new world that
was thrilling and full of adventure, a more perfect expression of life than a publican sitting and collecting unjust taxes. When Jesus invited him to become one of
his disciples, Matthew offered no excuses, no alibis, no
objection, not even the one we could all use of being
unworthy, a sinner. "He arose and followed him." He

was ready to give up everything else, even his sense of sin and self, to become the man Jesus saw.

Perhaps Peter may serve as a better example for many of us, since here we can see so clearly that victories in personal living are not won in a moment and character is not changed overnight. There are more recorded weaknesses of Peter than any other disciple. Peter, in the beginning, probably hated himself more than any of the others, because he knew himself so well. He undoubtedly thought there was no hope, and like most of us did not want to give up the way of life he had come to love, even though he disliked himself for loving it. He would climb, and slide, follow and love Jesus and the picture Jesus had of him, and then deny it all. Yet with all his shortcomings and instability, Peter became the man Jesus saw —Peter the Rock!

Peter is a shining example of hope to all of us who are discouraged over our shortcomings and failures. This disciple is our warrant to keep on trying even with the great gap we see between the perfection of the perfect Son, and our own lives.

After his ascension Jesus met Saul on the road to Damascus and the impact of that meeting gave Saul, the persecutor, whose hands were very literally stained with Christian blood, his first vision of the man he could become, the great Apostle Paul. Twelve centuries later Francesco de Pietro Bernardone, the fun loving, ordinary young son of a wealthy merchant in Assisi, faced a leper as he rode his horse up another dusty road. Fear and repugnance held the youth fast as he looked at the open sores, the frightful deterioration in the man before him. This was a normal reaction. But a picture warred within him, the picture of himself as he knew Jesus saw him. Before the picture could die away, young Francesco acted. Leaping from his horse he put all his money in the leper's hand and then kissed it. With that act Francesco de Pietro Bernardone, as he saw himself, gay lad about the town, erstwhile soldier, sinner surely in some measure, gave place before the man he was to become, and St. Francis of Assisi, the man Jesus saw in him, was born.

These are not ancient isolated examples. As we read the lives of the great ones we cannot fail to see that at some point they have ceased concentrating on a sinful self and become obedient to this loftier concept. There is no limit to it. When the Spirit of the Father moves, as it ever does, to fulfill itself through the Son, and man lets the Spirit work through him, we have Christ on the cross forgiving his enemies, Raphael painting the Sistine Madonna, Albert Schweitzer's adventures in Africa, Gandhi freeing a nation from bondage by a revolution of love.

This does not mean we should try to become religiously pious. This is often purely imitative. We cannot live another's demonstration. It is not that some people are religious and others are not, but only that it takes a lot of love to see in others, as well as in ourselves, the better self the Lord Jesus prophesied, who should do greater things than he did. Not, we note, the *same* things. This can be the glory of the Christian religion when rightly understood—there is a place for every personality, every temperament, every man, woman and child. No one is excluded unless he excludes himself.

As we set out on our own path of concentrating on ourselves as Jesus sees us, we will find we are following him, and are never alone. We can say with Paul, "I can do all things through Christ which strengtheneth me." If we are very faithful to the vision of what Jesus sees in us we may reach Paul's own climax, "I live; yet not I, but Christ liveth in me: and the life which I *now live in the flesh* (right here, not hereafter) I live by the faith of the Son of God, who loved *me,* and gave himself for *me.*"

This is to come as close as we can to the Perfect Man as we now understand him. Then we will know a more complete peace of body, mind and spirit than any we had dreamed. And it is within the reach of every one of us for the Grace of God goes with us on this journey.

15

WISDOM—ANCIENT
AND MODERN

PRAYER THERAPY IS NOT NEW. IT IS PROBABLY THE most ancient healing art known to man. On the other hand, it cannot be old. As each individual experiences true prayer within himself he releases a force as startling and modern as nuclear power.

In our studies we availed ourselves of the great wealth of literature open to all of us for inspiration, confirmation, and enlightenment. The Bible, of course, literally brims over with great, loving positive statements of truth. We found other sources as well and, in the remaining pages, are selected highlights which were particularly helpful. A list of the books from which these selections were gratefully borrowed follows to point the way for those who wish to continue to enlarge their horizons.

The selections represent the wisdom of many different theologies, of educators, scientists, physicians. We found that in dealing with spiritual matters truth was timeless, universal, and inter-faith. In order to follow clearly the way which unfolded to us in Prayer Therapy the material has been arranged according to specific chapters in this book. But here, from Fra Giovanni, A.D. 1513, are words of blessing and cheer extended to you, the individual reader:

No heaven can come to us unless our hearts
    Find rest in today. Take Heaven!
No peace lies in the future which is not hidden
    In this present little instant. Take peace!

> . . . . Life is so full of meaning and purpose,
>   So full of Beauty—beneath its covering—
> That you will find earth but cloaks your heaven.
>   Courage then to claim it: that is all!

The Kingdom Within

↗ "MAN IS SHUT UP INSIDE HIS MIND AND CANNOT STEP
  BEYOND IT."

"Such as men themselves are, such will God Himself seem to them to be."

John Smith, the Platonist

↗ THE WORLD OF CAUSES.

> "There is your world within.
>   There rid the dragons, root out the sin
> Your will is law in that small commonweal."

Gerard Manley Hopkins, 1844-1889
English Jesuit and poet

"People should think less about what they ought to do and more about what they ought to be. If only their being were good, their works would shine forth brightly."

Meister Johannes Eckhart, 1260-1327
German scholar, mystic

↗ KNOW THYSELF.

"One must be able to strip oneself of all self-deception, to see oneself naked to one's own eyes before one can come to terms with the elements of oneself and know who one really is."

Frances G. Wickes, 1882-
American psychotherapist

↗ THERE IS NO DECEPTION QUITE SO GREAT AS SELF-DE-
  CEPTION.

"In other living creatures ignorance of self is nature; in man it is vice."

Boethius 480?-?524
Roman philosopher

↗ MAKE PRAYER A PRACTICE IN HONESTY.

"A man has many skins in himself, covering the depths of his heart. Man knows so many things; he does not know himself. Why, thirty or forty skins or hides, just like an ox's or a bear's, so thick and hard, cover the soul. Go into your own ground and learn to know yourself there."

Meister Johannes Eckhart, 1260-1327

The Four Demons

↗ THE VICIOUS CIRCLE.

"It must be remembered that even though the Ego is the individual's inaccurate conception of himself, it seems to him to be what he is. It follows that all the thinking and striving of the egocentric person is basically concerned with avoiding all damage to his cherished Ego —his Seeming-self. He constantly fights against the breakdown of his Ego because its collapse seems to him to mean the destruction of his very Self, but even by these defensive efforts he inevitably brings about that breakdown which he dreads most. This is the result of the so-called vicious circle."

Fritz Kunkel, M.D., German psychotherapist &
Roy E. Dickerson, American author

"O make in me those civil wars to cease!"

Sir Philip Sidney, 1554-1586
English poet, statesman and soldier

"Beware of the emotions that are hosts to violence."

M.A.W.

↗ WHEN NEGATIVE FORCES RULE WITHIN.

"Something hath puddled his clear spirit. . . . And

in such cases, men's natures wrangle with inferior things, though great ones are their object."

William Shakespeare, 1564-1616
English poet, dramatist (Othello)

"If the doors of perception were cleansed, everything would appear to man as it is, infinite.

"For man has closed himself up, till he sees all things thro' narrow chinks in his cavern."

William Blake, 1757-1827
English poet, artist, mystic

↗ BONDAGE.

"A man is in bondage to whatever he cannot part with that is less than himself."

George Macdonald, 1824-1905
Scottish minister and writer

"By false desires and false thoughts man has built up for himself a false universe: as a mollusc, by the deliberate and persistent absorption of lime and rejection of all else, can build up for itself a hard shell which shuts it from the external world, and only represents in a distorted and unrecognizable form the ocean from which it was obtained. This hard and wholly unnutritious shell, this one-sided secretion of the surface-consciousness, makes as it were a little cave of illusion for each separate soul."

Evelyn Underhill, 1875-1944
English writer, mystic

↗ FEAR.

"Of primary importance in dealing with fear is the need of getting out into the open the object of our dread and frankly facing it. Human life is full of secret fears, thrust into the attics and dark corners of personality."

Harry Emerson Fosdick, 1878-
American clergyman

↗ NORMAL GUILT.

"She was sorely troubled with what is, by huge discourtesy, called a bad conscience—being in reality a conscience doing its duty so well that it makes the whole house uncomfortable."

George Macdonald, 1824-1905

↗ INFERIORITY FEELINGS.

"A sense of inferiority and inadequacy interferes with the attainment of your hopes, but self-confidence leads to self-realization and successful achievement. . . . It is appalling to realize the number of pathetic people who are hampered and made miserable by the malady popularly called the inferiority complex."

Norman Vincent Peale, 1898-
American clergyman

↗ MISGUIDED LOVE (HATE).

"Every thoughtful person who has ever considered the matter realizes that the doctors are right when they tell us that resentment, hate, grudge, ill will, jealousy, vindictiveness, are attitudes which produce ill-health. Have a fit of anger and experience for yourself that sinking feeling in the pit of your stomach, that sense of stomach sickness. Chemical reactions in the body are set up by emotional outbursts that result in feelings of ill-health. Should these be continued either violently or in a simmering state over a period of time, the general condition of the body will deteriorate."

Norman Vincent Peale, 1898-

The Healing Power

↗ GOD.

"I am thy holy Spirit of inspiration within thee, I am thy power to fulfill it."

Anonymous

"God is the natural appellation, for us Christians at least, for the supreme reality, so I will call this higher part of the universe by the name of God. We and God have business with each other; and in opening ourselves to his influence our deepest destiny is fulfilled. The universe, at those parts of it which our personal being constitutes, takes a turn genuinely for the worse or for the better in proportion as each one of us fulfills or evades God's demands."

William James, 1842-1910
American philosopher

"By love may He be gotten and holden, but by thought never."

The Cloud of Unknowing

↗ NECESSITY TO UNDERSTAND GOD AS LOVE.

"If then any child of the Father finds that he is afraid before Him, that the thought of God is a discomfort to Him, or even a terror, let him make haste—let him not linger to put on any garment, but rush at once in his nakedness, a true child, for shelter from his own evil and God's terror, into the salvation of the Father's arms."

George Macdonald, 1824-1905

↗ LOVE IS THE HEALING POWER.

"Love is infallible; it has no errors, for all errors are the want of love."

William Law, 1686-1761
English clergyman, mystic

"All externals must yield to love; for they are for the sake of love, and not love for them."

Hans Denk, 1495-1527
German mystic, spiritual reformer

"When God loves, He only desires to be loved, knowing that love will render all those who love Him happy."

St. Bernard, 1091-1153
French Abbot of Clairvaux

↗ WHERE IS GOD?

"It is foolish to seek for God outside of oneself. This will result either in idolatry or in scepticism."

Kagawa, 1888-
Japanese social reformer and evangelist

"Never wait for fitter time or place to talk to Him. To wait till thou go to church or to thy closet is to make Him wait. He will listen as thou walkest."

George Macdonald, 1824-1905

↗ NEED TO EXPERIENCE GOD WITHIN.

"All the great works and wonders that God has ever wrought . . . or even God Himself with all His goodness, can never make me blessed, but only in so far as they exist and are done and loved, known, tasted, and felt within me."

Theologia Germanica, 1497

↗ WHY WE MUST CONSCIOUSLY CHOOSE.

"God forces no one, for love cannot compel, and God's service, therefore, is a thing of perfect freedom."

Hans Denk, 1495-1527
German mystic, spiritual reformer

↗ THE MISSION OF CHRIST.

"For my part, I think the chief reason which prompted the invisible God to become visible in the flesh and to hold converse with men was to lead carnal men, who are only able to love carnally, to the healthful love of his flesh, and afterwards, little by little, to spiritual love."

St. Bernard, 1091-1153

↗ THE ART OF LOVING GOD.

"To love God with all our hearts and all our souls and all our minds means that every cleavage in human existence is overcome."

Reinhold Niebuhr, 1892-
American theologian, educator, author

"Some people want to see God with their eyes as they see a cow and to love him as they love their cow—they love their cow for the milk and cheese and profit it makes them."

Meister Johannes Eckhart, 1260-1327

"You will ask me questions how a man can give himself to that which he has no feeling of. especially when it relates to an Object which he does not see, nor never had acquaintance with? Sir. every day of your life you love things you do not see. Do you see for instance the wisdom of your friend? Do you see his sincerity, his disinterestedness, his virtue? You cannot see those objects with the eyes of the body, yet you prize and value them, and love them in that degree that you prefer them in your friend to riches. and outward beauty. and to everything that strikes the eye. Love then the wisdom and supreme goodness of God, as you love the wisdom and imperfect goodness of your friend. And if you cannot presently have a sensible feeling of love, you at least may have a love of preference in your will and desire, which is the essential point."

François Fénelon, 1651-1715
French Archbishop of Cambray

"Temperance is love surrendering itself wholly to Him who is its object; courage is love bearing all things gladly for the sake of Him who is its object; justice is love serving only Him who is its object. and therefore rightly ruling; prudence is love making wise distinctions between what hinders and what helps itself."

St. Augustine, 354-430
Latin Church Father

⌐ LOVE OF NEIGHBOR.

"By love I do not mean any natural tenderness, which is more or less in people according to their constitution; but I mean a larger principle of the soul, founded in

reason and piety, which makes us tender, kind and gentle
to all our fellow creatures of God, and for his sake."

William Law, 1686-1761
English clergyman, mystic

"A man must not choose his neighbor: he must take
the neighbor that God sends him. . . . The love of our
neighbor is the only door out of the dungeon of self,
where we mope and mow, striking sparks, and rubbing
phosphorescences out of the walls, and blowing our own
breath in our own nostrils instead of issuing to the fair
sunlight of God, the sweet winds of the universe."

George Macdonald, 1824-1905

⚡ THOU SHALT LOVE THYSELF PROPERLY.

"It is one of the great discoveries of modern psychology that our attitudes toward ourselves are just as
complicated as our attitudes toward others—sometimes
more so. The great commandment of religion, 'Thou
shalt love thy neighbor as thyself,' might now be better
interpreted to mean, 'Thou shalt love thyself properly,
and then thou wilt love thy neighbor.' . . .

"This condemnation of selfishness and exaltation of
altruism is the traditional attitude of religion. It holds up
a worthy goal to be sure, but there are many errors in
its estimate of human nature. Is it true that we are spontaneously good to ourselves? The evidence points in quite
the opposite direction. Men may wish to be good to
themselves, but how misguided and unwise they are in
their attempts to reach that goal! The fact is that we often
treat ourselves more rigidly, more fanatically, more venge-
fully, than we do others. Suicide, self-mutilation, and
more subtle forms of self-degradation such as alcoholism,
drug addiction, and promiscuity are pitiful proofs of
this. Such self-hate is not restricted to the weak and the
insane. Violent forms of aggression against the self occur
daily and less dramatically in the lives of ordinary men
and women.

"He who hates himself, who does not have proper regard for his own capacities, powers, compassions, actually can have no respect for others. Deep within himself he will hate his brothers when he sees in them his own marred image. Love for oneself is the foundation of a brotherly society and personal peace of mind. By loving oneself I do not mean coddling oneself, indulging in vanity, conceit, self-glorification. I do, however, insist on the necessity of a proper self-regard as a prerequisite of the good and the moral life.

"Psychology reveals the underlying causes of false self-love and destructive self-hatred. Religion, allied with psychology, can demonstrate just what true self-regard means.

"Theoretically, religion has always been concerned with the achievement of true self-love. It eternally proclaims the value of every human personality, the sanctity of every man. But it has been strangely impotent to implement that sanctity. All the streets of the world are teeming with men and women who mutilate themselves spiritually and mentally in the invisible ways of self-criticism and self-degradation. . . .

"It is important that all of us become wise enough to recognize where we go astray in our attitudes toward ourselves and how we become enslaved to false notions of what we are and what we ought to be. Some of us think we are loving ourselves when we are really strangling or suffocating ourselves with morbid self-concern. We maintain a cruel contempt for our own capabilities and virtues or become unconscious victims of a paralyzing egocentricity. When we free ourselves from that false self-love which is narcissism, that destructive self-hatred which is masochism, we become for the first time integrated enough to become friendly with ourselves and with others. We are on the road to proper self-love. Such self-love implies many things, but above everything else it is rooted in self-respect. And no man or woman can have self-respect unless he has learned the art of renunciation and the equally vital art of self-acceptance."

Joshua Loth Liebman, 1907-
Jewish rabbi, educator

"You are a distinct portion of the essence of God; and contain part of him in yourself. Why. then, are you ignorant of your noble birth? Why do you not consider whence you came? Why do you not remember, when you are eating, who you are who eat; and whom you feed? Do you not know that it is the Divine you feed? The Divine you exercise? You carry a God about with you, poor wretch, and know nothing of it."

Epictetus, A.D. 60
Greek philosopher

How to Cast Out Demons

↗ THE NEED FOR PRAYER.

"Reader, if you are in any trouble, try whether God will not help you: if you are in no need, why should you ask questions about prayer? True, he knows little of himself who does not know that he is wretched, and miserable, and poor, and blind, and naked; but until he begins at least to suspect a need, how can he pray?"

George Macdonald, 1824-1905

↗ PRAY REGULARLY.

"Question. What is it to believe in the light?"

"Answer. To receive its testimony either concerning good or evil, and so either to turn towards or from, in the will and power which the light begets in the heart."

"Question. How will this save me?"

"Answer. By this means; that in thee which destroys thee, and separates thee from the living God, is daily wrought out, and the heart daily changed into the image of him who is light, and brought into unity and fellowship with the light possessing of it, and being possessed by it; and this is salvation.

"It brings peace, joy, and glory. Faith in the light breaks down the wall of darkness, the wall of partition, that which separates from the peace, that which causeth the anguish and trouble upon the soul, and so brings into peace."

Isaac Pennington, 1616-1679
Quaker leader

"He who interrupts the course of his spiritual exercises and prayer is like a man who allows a bird to escape from his hand; he can hardly catch it again."

St. John of the Cross, 1542-1591
Spanish mystic

"If the heart wanders or is distracted, bring it back to the point quite gently and replace it tenderly in its Master's presence. And even if you did nothing during the whole of your hour but bring your heart back and place it again in Our Lord's presence, though it went away every time you brought it back, your hour would be very well employed."

St. Francis de Sales, 1567-1622
French Archbishop of Geneva

"Our safety does not lie in the present perfection of our knowledge of the will of God, but in our sincerity in obeying the light we have, and in seeking for more."

Edward Worsdell, 1853-1908
English teacher

↗ PRAYER AS AN ACT OF SURRENDER.

"God is bound to act, to pour Himself into thee as soon as He shall find thee ready."

Meister Johannes Eckhart, 1260-1327

"God wants only one thing in the whole world, the thing which it needs; . . . that thing is to find the innermost part of the noble spirit of man clean and ready for Him to accomplish the divine purpose therein. He has all power in heaven and earth, but the power to do His work in man against man's will, He has not got."

Johann Tauler, 1304?-1361
German friar-preacher

"We think we must climb to a certain height of goodness before we can reach God. But He says not 'At the end of the end of the way you may find me'; He says 'I am the Way; I am the road under your feet, the road that begins just as low as you happen to be.' If we are in a hole the Way begins in the hole. The moment we set our face in the same direction as His, we are walking with God."

Helen Wodehouse, 1880-
Educator

"There is no escape. There is no heaven with a little of hell in it—no plan to retain this or that of the devil in our hearts or our pockets. Our Satan must go, every hair and feather!"

George Macdonald, 1824-1905

⤢ MAKE PRAYER POSITIVE.
"But open your eyes and the world is full of God."

Jacob Boehme, 1575-1624
German mystic

"What is't to live, if not to pull the strings
Of thought that pull those grosser strings whereby
We pull our limbs to pull material things
Into such shapes as in our thoughts doth lie?"

Samuel Butler, 1835-1902
English author

"When we look at our world with the eyes of the mind, freshened by divine insights as Christ would have us, we see things with a positive rather than a negative outlook. Consider any local community. One man lives in that town with a negative, critical attitude. He sees the pettiness of its people, the stodginess of the place, all the tawdry things that Sinclair Lewis portrayed in 'Main Street.' Another man lives in the town, and sees the heartiness of its neighborly spirit, the opportunities offered by its schools and churches, all the inviting things that a William Allen White would see in his community. It is the same town; the difference is in the set of the mental focus and the depth of insight."

Ralph W. Sockman, 1889-
American clergyman

↗ POSITIVE PRAYER AND POSITIVE DEEDS.

"The right relation between prayer and conduct is not that conduct is supremely important and prayer may help it, but that prayer is supremely important and conduct tests it."

William Temple, 1881-1944
English Archbishop of Canterbury

↗ CHOOSING OUR TRUE DESIRES.

"You are as holy as you will to be."

Jan van Ruysbroeck, 1293-1381
Flemish mystical theologian

"God did not deprive thee of the operation of His love, but thou didst deprive Him of thy cooperation."

St. Francis de Sales, 1567-1622

↗ RECEPTIVITY.

"His giving is my taking."

Meister Johannes Eckhart, 1260-1327

↗ WHY WE CAN RECEIVE "IMMEDIATELY."

"He brought light out of darkness, not out of a lesser light; he can bring thy summer out of winter, though thou have no spring; though in the ways of fortune or understanding or conscience, thou have been benighted till now, wintered and frozen, clouded and eclipsed, damped and benumbed, smothered and stupefied till now, now God comes to thee, not as in the dawning of the day, not as in the bud of the spring, but as the sun at noon."

John Donne, 1573-1631
English poet, divine

↗ ACCEPTING FORGIVENESS.

"Saints are men who permit God's forgiveness to come into them so fully that not only are their sins washed out, but also their very selves, their egos, and the root of their self-will. And again, we see. the intensity of their power really to forgive is in exact proportion to the degree that they have permitted themselves to be forgiven and so brought back to God. Look for a moment at the quality of their forgiveness, what they have accepted from God and so may pass on to man. I forgive to the level that I have been forgiven, and if that level is moderate (because I made reservations in what I declared, because I only wanted to lose my vices and not myself), I can forgive only people who have offended moderately and my forgiveness helps them only moderately. If I try forgiving people who have wronged me or others intensely. I find either I can't do it at all or the quality of my forgiveness is so weak that it is either resented (as the maniac became more fierce as the disciples tried to cure him) or more often dismissed with contempt. We have not power on earth to forgive sins because we are not forgiven to that degree—to that degree that God is our sole end and our ego is no more. . . .

"If, then, we are to save our social life, we must produce men so deeply forgiven that they can at least forgive, creatively discharge with a renewed will, give the conviction of new unlimited kinship and friendship to those extreme types of public enmity which our social system is producing."

Anonymous

↗ RECEIVING INSPIRATION AND GUIDANCE.

"Listen to God in silence when we have spoken to Him, for He speaks in His turn during prayer."

John Peter de Caussade d.1751

How to Evaluate Yourself

↗ PRELUDE TO PRAYER.

"As light increases, we see ourselves to be worse than we thought. We are amazed at our former blindness as we see issuing forth from the depths of our heart a whole swarm of shameful feelings, like filthy reptiles crawling from a hidden cave. We never could have believed that we had harboured such things, and we stand aghast as we watch them gradually appear. But we must neither be amazed nor disheartened. We are not worse than we were; on the contrary, we are better. But while our faults diminish, the light by which we see them waxes brighter, and we are filled with horror. Bear in mind, for your comfort, that we only perceive our malady when the cure begins."

François Fénelon, 1651-1715

↗ OUR CONSCIOUSNESS WILL NOT BE REBUILT IN A NIGHT.

"As the world must be redeemed in a few men to begin with, so the soul is redeemed in a few of its thoughts and works and ways to begin with: It takes a long time to finish the new creation of this redemption."

George Macdonald, 1824-1905

"Self-love cannot endure to see itself; it would die of shame and vexation! If by chance it gets a glimpse, it at once places itself in some artificial light, so as to soften the full hideousness and find some comfort. And so there will always be some remains of self-delusion clinging to us while we still cling to self and its imperfections. Before we can see ourselves truly, self-love must be rooted up, and the love of God alone move us; and then the same light which showed us our faults would cure them. Till then we only know ourselves by halves, because we are only half God's, and hold a great deal more to ourselves than we imagine or choose to see. When the truth has taken full possession of us, we shall see clearly, and then we shall behold ourselves without partiality or flattery, as we see our neighbors. Meanwhile God spares our weakness, by only showing us our own deformity by degrees, and as He gives strength to bear the sight. He only shows us to ourselves, so to say, by bits; here one and there another, as He undertakes our correction."

François Fénelon, 1651-1715

↗ RULES FOR OUR INNER JOURNEY.

"We must start without delay on the painful, steep, humiliating path of undoing our busy, deliberately deluded selves. So only will the Kingdom come, where it must come fully and where we alone can decide whether it shall come—in ourselves. 'The Kingdom of God is within you,' yes, but only if we are prepared to let that powerful germ of eternal life grow, until it splits away and consumes this husk, our ego. . . .

"That, then, is the first step, known by the grim technical term, purgation. I must start with myself, and stay with myself until some intention appears in my actions, some consistency between what I say and do. I must not escape into denunciation, coercion, or even superior concern for anyone else. I shall do so if I can; that is the invariable trick of the ego, trying to escape and save itself from its necessary death."

Gerald Heard, 1889-
English author, religious philosopher

↗ DEFENSE MECHANISMS.

"Many are the devices and marvelous the elaborations by which men everywhere seek to avoid condemnation before that inner tribunal known as conscience. To be at one with that which is supreme in our hierarchy of loyalties, that to which men generally give the name of God, is ever essential to mental health; to be isolated or estranged through the consciousness that there is that

within which we cannot acknowledge without being condemned means mental disorder and spiritual death."

Anton T. Boisen, 1876-
American educator, theologian

↗ LOOK BACKWARD.

"No one is born a new being. He bears in his psyche
the imprint of past generations. He is a combination of
ancestral units from which a new being must be fused,
yet he also bears within him an essential germ a potential
of a unique individual value. The discovery of this unique
essence and its development is the quest of consciousness."

Frances G. Wickes, 1882-

↗ LOOK INWARD.

"A splendid freedom awaits us when we realize that
we need not feel like moral lepers or emotional pariahs
because we have some aggressive, hostile thoughts and
feelings toward ourselves and others. When we acknowledge these feelings we no longer have to pretend to
be that which we are not."

Joshua Loth Liebman, 1907-

↗ LOOK OUTWARD.

"A Christian may believe in all the sacred figures and
yet remain undeveloped and unchanged in his innermost
soul, for he sees the 'whole God outside' and does not
experience him in his own soul. His decisive motives,
interests and impulses do not come from the sphere of
Christianity, but from the unconscious and undeveloped
soul, which is just as pagan and archaic as ever. The
truth of this statement is not only evident in the life of
the individual but also in the sum total of individual
lives the people. The great events of our world, which
are planned and carried out by men, do not breathe the
spirit of Christianity but of unadorned paganism."

Carl G. Jung, M.D., 1875-1961
Swiss psychiatrist

↗ Look onward.

"The true self-sacrifice is the one that sacrifices the hidden thing in the self which would work harm to ourselves and to others. It is an effort to become more and more conscious of all the forces in the unconscious, of the unworthy personal motives that work underground, as well as the inherited forces, so that our lives shall become more and more full of understanding and of really conscious choice. In this way we do 'descend into hell,' the depth of the unconscious where lie all those things that would destroy our conscious attitude and which we most fear to face and acknowledge. From such a descent can come a new life if the new understanding is accepted by the individual. . . .

"Our greatest task is to have the courage to face the thing that rises in us, whether it take the form of doubt which must be thought out, or the knowledge of the unacceptable thing in ourselves with which we must reckon. In this way only can be found the acceptance of greater consciousness."

Frances G. Wickes, 1882-

↗ Meeting the demands of life.

"Every person has a choice of three levels on which to live. He can be childish, ego-centric, and soft in mind, fondly imagining that the world revolves around his small desire. . . . That is the lowest level.

"Against this shallow innocence those on the second level energetically rebel. Some go fascist; others go communist or Pharisee. For the sake of future order or brotherhood, let there be violence now. That the Kingdom of Heaven may come according to my specifications, away with anybody who chooses a method different from that of my party. . . .

"On the third level move those athletes of the spirit who are fundamentally effective and aware . . . Level number three is always patronized by level number two as though it were only level number one. The communist brushes Kagawa aside as a peddler of religious opium; the sword-fondling nationalist labels Gandhi as a sentimentalist who only turns the other cheek; the half-baked intellectual mutters that Schweitzer is a fool for leaving the popular lecture room to bury himself in Africa. Yet Kagawa, Gandhi, and Schweitzer are more poignantly aware of ultimate reality than inhibited atheists are. They cherish a deeper attachment to native land than arrogant nationalists can feel. They have a wider grasp of philosophy, by being brotherly. than the inhibited intellectuals in their ivory towers ever reach. . . .

"Theirs is the gift of making others feel at home because they are themselves at ease with life. . . .

"Not every moment, but oftener than we, they breathe and dream in union with the deepest law of human life. It is a law that Jesus proclaimed again and again and embodied all the time: If any man tries to defend himself he will be lost but if he throws all of himself into the cause of the family of God he will find his soul." (abridged)

Allan A. Hunter, 1893-
American minister, author

Prayer Therapy on a Daily Basis

↗ SYMPTOMS AND SUFFERING.

"Our greatest hope is in this, that suffering is there. It is the language of imperfection. Its very utterance carries in it the trust in the perfect. like the baby's cry which would be dumb if it had no faith in the mother."

Rabindranath Tagore, 1861-1941
Indian poet, dramatist, novelist

"We suffer, yet do not allow the mission of suffering to be accomplished in us. I pray the Lord that we may none of us fall into that torpid state in which our crosses do us no good."

François Fénelon, 1651-1715

"But now these symptoms which seemed to be bad and inimical, namely, this anxiety or guilt, prove themselves to be helpful and friendly, for they intrude themselves in order to bring healing by awakening this living yet unalive person. They are the voice of this life which is not lived, and their force is the power of life itself. They are the messengers of the We which represents this power of life, even within the egocentric mind."

Fritz Kunkel, 1889-

↗ THE WAY IN PRAYER THERAPY

"Cleanse your own heart, cast out from your mind pain, fear, envy, ill-will, avarice, cowardice, passion uncontrolled. These things you cannot cast out unless you look to God alone; on him alone set your thoughts, and consecrate yourself to his commands. If you wish for anything else, with groaning and sorrow you will follow what is stronger than you, ever seeking peace outside you, and never able to be at peace; for you seek it where it is not, and refuse to seek it where it is."

Epictetus, A.D. 60

↗ MEDITATION AND LOVE.

"Contemplation is a perception of God or of divine things; simple, free, penetrating, certain, proceeding from love and tending to Love."

Louis Lallemant, 1587-1635

↗ DEALING WITH FEAR.

"We reviewed our fears thoroughly. We put them on paper, even though we had no resentment in connection with them. We asked ourselves why we had them. Wasn't it because self-reliance failed us? Self-reliance was good as far as it went, but it didn't go far enough. Some of us once had great self-confidence, but it didn't fully solve the fear problem, or any other. When it made us cocky, it was worse.

"Perhaps there is a better way—we think so. For we are now on a different basis; the basis of trusting and relying upon God. We trust infinite God rather than our finite selves. We are in the world to play the role He assigns. Just to the extent that we do as we think He would have us, and humbly rely on Him, does He enable us to match calamity with serenity.

"We never apologize to anyone for depending upon our Creator. We can laugh at those who think spirituality the way of weakness. Paradoxically, it is the way of strength. The verdict of the ages is that faith means courage. All men of faith have courage. They trust their God. We never apologize for God. Instead we let Him demonstrate, through us, what He can do. We ask Him to remove our fear and direct our attention to what He would have us be. At once, we commence to outgrow fear."

Alcoholics Anonymous

↗ DEALING WITH HATRED.

"If the desire to be honest is greater than the desire to be "good" or "bad," then the terrific power of one's vices will become clear. And behind the vice the old forgotten fear will come up (the fear of being excluded from life) and behind the fear the pain (the pain of not being loved) and behind this pain of loneliness the deepest and most profound and most hidden of all human desires: the desire to love and to give oneself in love and to be part of the living stream we call brotherhood. And the moment love is discovered behind hatred all hatred disappears."

Fritz Kunkel, 1889-

↗ GETTING SELF OUT OF THE WAY.

"The difference between a good and a bad man does not lie in this, that the one wills that which is good and the other does not, but solely in this, that the one concurs with the living inspiring spirit of God within him, and the other resists it. and can be chargeable with evil only because he resists it."

William Law, 1686-1761

↗ INSISTING ON A RE-ACTION.

"As we go through the day, we pause when agitated or doubtful, and ask for the right thought or action. We constantly remind ourselves we are no longer running the show, humbly saying to ourselves many times each day 'Thy will be done.' We are then in much less danger of excitement, fear, anger, worry, self-pity, or foolish decisions. We become much more efficient. We do not tire so easily, for we are not burning up energy foolishly as we did when trying to arrange life to suit ourselves. It works—it really does."

Alcoholics Anonymous

↗ RICHER, FULLER LIVING THROUGH MORNING AND EVENING PRAYER.

"Immediately you awake set your first thought on God. Keep your mind on him for a few seconds. Do not think of him subjectively, as to your relation to him, your failures, your sins, or your needs, but rather objectively. Let your whole self become conscious of him. Think of him as shining beauty, radiant joy, creative power, all-pervading love, perfect understanding, purity, and serenity. This need only take a moment or two once the habit has been formed, but it is of inestimable importance. It sets the tone for the whole day. . . .

"One's waking mood tends to correspond to the state of mind in which one falls asleep. If, therefore, as a result of a disturbed night or simply because of lack of practice, this first thought of God should evade you, look out of the window for something obviously made by him, trees, flowers, the sky, or a wind-shaped cloud, even a gray one, and ponder on the perfection of his handicraft. . . .

"Never get into bed with a burdened or a heavy mind; whether it be a vague oppression or a definite fear, shame or remorse, anger or hate, get rid of the evil thing before you lie down to sleep. Night is a holy time, a time of renewing and refreshment. He giveth to His beloved while they sleep; our unconscious mind is active during our slumber. Settle down restfully to let your mind get clear and your spirit unclogged."

Muriel Lester, 1883-
English author, social worker

"Your enjoyment of the world is never right till every morning you awake in Heaven; see yourself in your Father's palace; and look upon the skies, the earth and the air as celestial joys; having such a reverend esteem of all, as if you were among the Angels. The bride of a monarch, in her husband's chamber, hath no such causes of delight as you."

Thomas Traherne, 1637?-1674
English poet, religious writer

"I don't like the man who doesn't sleep, says God.
Sleep is the friend of man.
Sleep is the friend of God.
Sleep is perhaps the most beautiful thing I have created.
And I myself rested on the seventh day.
He whose heart is pure, sleeps. And he who sleeps has a
    pure heart.
That is the great secret of being as indefatigable as a
    child.
Of having that strength in the legs that a child has.
Those new legs, those new souls,
And to begin afresh every morning, ever new,
Like young hope, new hope.
But they tell me that there are men
Who work well and sleep badly.
Who don't sleep. What a lack of confidence in me."

Charles Péguy, 1873-1914
French writer, mystic

↗ PRAYING FOR THE WORLD.

"The more a man becomes conscious of himself through self-knowledge and its corresponding effect upon action, there is an increasing tendency for that layer of the personal unconscious that has overlaid the collective unconscious to disappear. In this way a conscious function is born. that is no longer imprisoned in the petty, oversensitive, and personal world of the ego, but participates freely in the wider world of objective interests. This extended consciousness ceases to be a knot of personal wishes, fears, hopes and ambitions that have always to be compensated or corrected by unconscious. personal counter-tendencies. Instead, it now becomes a function of relation that is linked up with the world of objects. and by which the individual is pledged to an unconditioned, responsible, and indissoluble intercourse with the world. The complications that belong to this stage are no longer egoistic wish-conflicts. but difficulties that concern others just as much as oneself."

Carl G. Jung, M.D., 1875-1961
Swiss psychiatrist

↗ PRAYING FOR OTHERS.

"Intercession is a great and necessary part of Christian Devotion. The first followers of Christ seem to support all their love, and to maintain all their intercourse and correspondence. by mutual prayers for one another. This was the ancient friendship of Christians, uniting and cementing their hearts.

"A frequent intercession with God. earnestly beseeching him to forgive the sins of all mankind, to bless them with his providence, enlighten them with his Spirit, and bring them to everlasting happiness, is the divinest exercise that the heart of man can be engaged in."

William Law, 1686-1761

"Our prayer for others ought never to be: 'God! give them the light Thou hast given to me!' but: 'Give them all the light and truth they need for their highest development!' "

Mahatma Gandhi, 1869-1948
Indian statesman, national leader

↗ PRAYING FOR OUR ENEMIES.

"And so throughout eternity
I forgive you, you forgive me;
As our dear Redeemer said,
This is the Wine, this is the Bread."

William Blake, 1757-1827

"If I hate or despise any one man in the world, I hate something that God cannot hate, and despise that which he loves. And though many people may appear to us ever so sinful, odious, or extravagant in their conduct, we must never look upon that, as the least motive for any contempt or disregard of them; but look upon them with the greater compassion, as being in the most pitiable condition that can be."

William Law, 1686-1761

↗ EXAMINING TRUE DESIRES.

"What is man? An angel, an animal, a void, a world, a nothing surrounded by God, indigent of God, capable of God, filled with God, if it so desires."

Pierre de Berulle, 1575-1629
French Cardinal

"The seed of God is in us. Given an intelligent and hardworking farmer, it will thrive and grow up to God, whose seed it is; and accordingly its fruits will be God-nature. Pear seeds grow into pear trees, nut seeds into nut trees, and God seed into God."

Meister Johannes Eckhart, 1260-1327

↗ BEING ALONE WITH GOD AND SELF.

"By all means use sometimes to be alone,
Salute thyself: see what thy soul doth wear.
Dare to look in thy chest: for 'tis thy own:

And tumble up and down what thou find'st there.
Who cannot rest till he good fellows find,
He breaks up house, turns out of doors his mind."
                                    George Herbert, 1593-1632
                                    English religious poet, writer

↗ SAYING A DEFINITE "NO" AND A DEFINITE "YES."

"Instead of asking yourself whether you believe or
not, ask yourself whether you have this day done one
thing because He said, 'Do it,' or once abstained because
He said 'Do not do it.' It is simply absurd to say you believe, or even want to believe, in Him, if you do not
anything He tells you."
                                    George Macdonald, 1824-1905

↗ THE PERFECT MAN.

"Man impelled by his natural foresight inclines toward
his own perfection."
                                    Dante Alighieri, 1265-1321
                                    Italian poet

"Hope holds to Christ the mind's own mirror out
To take His lovely likeness more and more."
                                    Gerard Manley Hopkins, 1844-1889

"Knowledge of ourselves teaches us whence we come,
where we are and whither we are going. We come from
God and we are in exile; and it is because our potency of
affection tends toward God that we are aware of this state
of exile."
                                    Jan van Ruysbroeck, 1293-1381

"When we receive His image into our spiritual mirror, He enters with it. Our thought is not cut off from
His. Our open receiving thought is His door to come in.
When our hearts turn to Him, that is opening the door
to Him, that is holding up our mirror to Him; then He
comes in, not by our thought only, not in our idea only,

but He comes Himself and of His own will—comes in as we could not take Him, but as He can come."

George Macdonald, 1824-1905

"His likeness to Christ is the truth of a man, even as the perfect meaning of a flower is the truth of a flower. . . . As Christ is the blossom of humanity, so the blossom of every man is the Christ perfected in him."

George Macdonald, 1824-1905

APPENDIX

(A List of Acknowledgments and Suggested Reading.)

WE HAVE SPOKEN OF THE READING THAT ASSISTED Prayer Therapy students to develop positive, lofty concepts. Chapter 15, "Wisdom—Ancient and Modern," can do no more than give the reader a sample of the vast storehouse of inspiration available.

Perhaps the easiest way to become acquainted with some of the wisdom of the ages is to take advantage of the dedicated work already done by those who have given us excellent anthologies. Among these, the authors are indebted to the work done by Dorothy Berkley Phillips, editor of *The Choice Is Always Ours,* publisher Richard R. Smith, Rindge, New Hampshire, 1954 and Aldous Huxley, *The Perennial Philosophy,* Harper & Brothers, New York, 1945. C. S. Lewis has done a slim volume of excerpts from the writings and sermons of George Macdonald: *George Macdonald: An Anthology,* Macmillan, 1948, and Mary Strong, who edited *Letters of the Scattered Brotherhood,* Harper & Brothers, New York, 1948, has made interesting use of fine quotes between these inspirational letters.

We wish to acknowledge with gratitude permission from the following publishers and individuals to reprint selections from their copyrighted works.

Abingdon-Cokesbury Press. THE HIGHER HAPPINESS, by Ralph W. Sockman, copyright 1950.

Abingdon-Cokesbury Press, WAYS OF PRAYING, by Muriel Lester, copyright 1932.

Association Press, THREE TRUMPETS SOUND, by Allan A. Hunter.

Baillere, Tindall and Cox, London, TWO ESSAYS ON ANALYTICAL PSYCHOLOGY, by Carl G. Jung, translation by H. G. and C. F. Baynes.

Charles Scribner's and Sons, HOW CHARACTER DEVELOPS, by Fritz Kunkel and Roy E. Dickerson, copyright 1940.

Charles Scribner's and Sons, IN SEARCH OF MATURITY, by Fritz Kunkel, copyright 1943.

Harper & Brothers, New York, AN INTERPRETATION OF CHRISTIAN ETHICS, by Reinhold Niebuhr, copyright 1935.

Harper & Brothers, New York, THE CREED OF CHRIST, by Gerald Heard, copyright 1940.

Harper & Brothers, New York, THE EXPLORATION OF THE INNER WORLD, by Anton T. Boisen, copyright 1936.

Harper & Brothers, New York, KAGAWA, by William Axling, copyright 1932.

Harper & Brothers, New York, MAN THE UNKNOWN, by Alexis Carrel, copyright 1935.

Harper & Brothers, New York, ON BEING A REAL PERSON, by Harry Emerson Fosdick.

John Day Company, Inc., THE DISCOVERY OF IN-DIA, by Jawaharlal Nehru, copyright 1946.

Longmans, Green and Co., Inc., VARIETIES OF RELI-GIOUS EXPERIENCE, by William James.

The Macmillan Company, PERSONALITY, by Rabin-dranath Tagore.

Methuen and Co., Ltd., MYSTICISM, by Evelyn Un-derhill.

Pantheon Books Inc., New York, GOD SPEAKS, by Charles Péguy, copyright 1945.

Prentice-Hall, Inc., THE SPRINGS OF SILENCE, by Madeline DeFrees, copyright 1953.

Rinehart & Co., Inc., THE INNER WORLD OF MAN, by Frances G. Wickes, copyright 1936.

Simon and Schuster, Inc., PEACE OF MIND, by Joshua Loth Liebman, copyright 1946.

Trubner & Co., Inc., Ltd., PSYCHOLOGY AND AL-CHEMY, by Carl G. Jung, translation by Barbara Han-nah.

Works Publishing Inc., New York, ALCOHOLICS ANONYMOUS, copyright 1951.

INDEX

243

How to raise a brighter child

These new methods, based on the theories of famous physicians, educators and behavioral scientists, are simple and fun—and they can increase your child's I. Q. by 20 points or more! Start using them as early as possible—even right after birth!

Imagine a 21-month-old with a reading vocabulary of 160 words...a boy of four who enjoys teaching himself major number principles...a girl not yet four who reads at the third grade level! None of these children was born a genius. Yet, through the early learning concepts described in this remarkable new book—HOW TO RAISE A BRIGHTER CHILD—all are being helped to develop above-average intelligence and a joyous love of learning.

Now you can give your little pre-schooler the same happy advantages...and they may well last throughout your child's life. For according to recent research, a child's I. Q. level is not permanently fixed at birth. It can be raised—or lowered by 20 points or even more in the precious years before six, by the way you rear your child at home.

Take the book now for a 30-day FREE trial

Send now for your copy of HOW TO RAISE A BRIGHTER CHILD. When it arrives, turn to the section that applies to your child *right now*, at this particular stage in his life. Apply some of the early learning techniques it shows you how to use. Then if not convinced this one book can make a world of difference in your child's mental development, return it within 30 days and owe nothing. If you decide to keep the book, it is yours for only $5.95 plus a small mailing charge. Take advantage of this opportunity! See your bookseller or mail the coupon today.

Joan Beck is known by millions of readers who follow her syndicated column, "You And Your Child." A graduate of Northwestern University, holding Bachelor's and Master's degrees, she has received several academic and professional awards and honors. She is married to Ernest W. Beck, a medical illustrator. They have two children, aged 15 and 12.